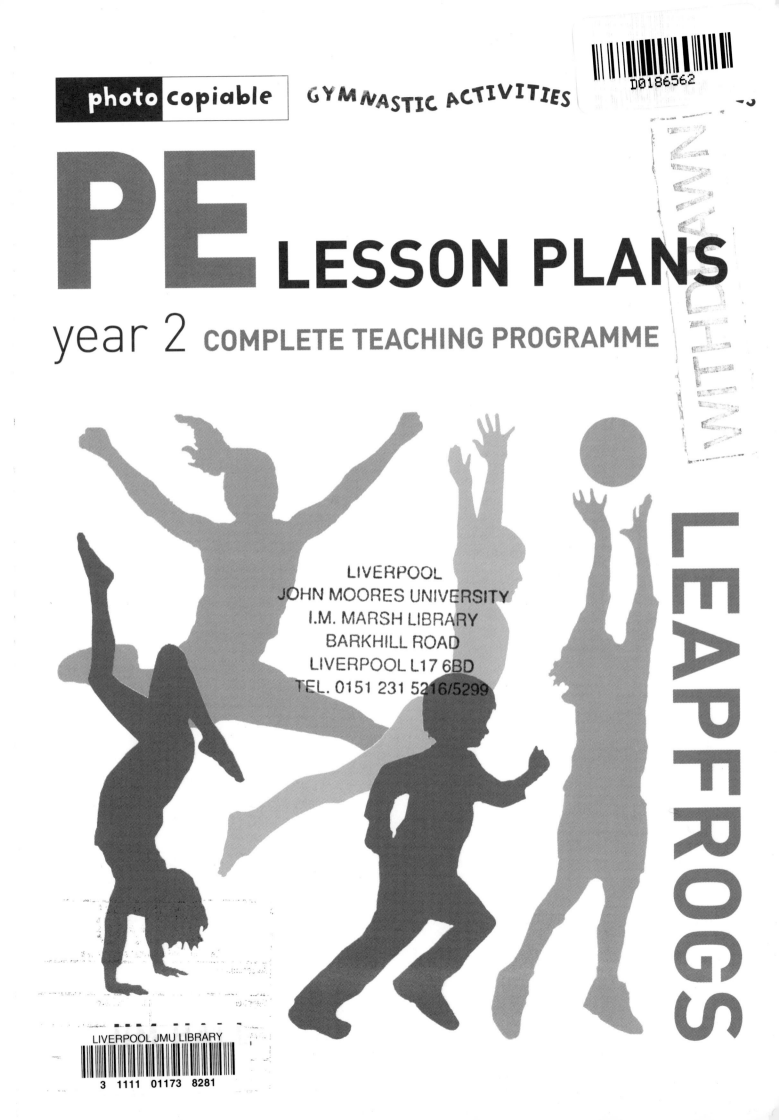

GYMNASTIC ACTIVITIES

# PE LESSON PLANS

## year 2 COMPLETE TEACHING PROGRAMME

WITH

LEAPFROGS

Published in 2005 by A & C Black Publishers Ltd
37 Soho Square, London W1D 3QZ
www.acblack.com

ISBN 0 7136 7213 7

A CIP record for this book is available from the British Library.

Note: While every effort has been made to ensure that the content of this book is as technically accurate and as sound as possible, neither the author nor the publisher can accept responsibility for any injury or loss sustained as a result of the use of this material.

A & C Black uses paper produced with elemental chlorine-free pulp, harvested from managed sustainable forests.

**Acknowledgements**
Cover and inside design by Peter Bailey
Illustrations by Eleanor King

Typeset in 10pt DIN Regular.

Printed and bound in Great Britain by Martins the Printers, Berwick upon Tweed.

# Contents

# Introduction

Good lesson plans and a sense of staff unity regarding the 'Why?' 'What?' and 'How?' of Physical Education are essential to a successful programme with high standards and continuity from year to year. Included in this book is a year's worth of lesson plans and detailed accompanying notes to help with the 'Why?' 'What?' and 'How?' It is hoped that these user-friendly lesson plans and notes will also contribute to the development of a sense of staff-room togetherness in a belief in the value of, and a desire to apply good practice in, Physical Education.

A pupil's all-round educational development is at its most intense during the infant school years and Physical Education makes unique and valuable contributions to this:

○ **physical** development comes from lively participation in all the natural activities of running, jumping, landing, climbing, rolling, balancing, taking weight on to the hands, lifting and carrying light apparatus, chasing, dodging, and playing with a wide variety of games implements;

○ **social** development comes from sharing hall and playground space unselfishly with others, demonstrating to help others learn if called upon, watching and commenting appreciatively on others' performances, taking turns, and helping others to lift and carry apparatus;

○ **emotional** development comes from enjoying a sense of pleasure from participation in natural activities, feeling better about oneself after being praised for good work, and getting rid of surplus energy, which is normal in young, naturally active children. Such release is now denied to many young children whose lifestyles are becoming more sedentary and less physical;

○ **intellectual** development accompanies the gaining of knowledge and understanding about ways of moving and controlling our bodies. Children will begin to make judgements about themselves in the space being shared with others.

The stimulation of almost non-stop, vigorous and enjoyable activity should be the most important feature and aim of Physical Education, ideally inspired by enthusiastic teachers who value the subject. Working in a hall or playground with apparatus, wide spaces, rapidly moving pupils and safety and behaviour considerations to manage, is a problem, particularly for teachers with limited training in teaching Physical Education. This book aims to help teachers by providing information, ideas and practical help with planning, teaching and developing their Gymnastic Activities, Dance and Games lessons. It also aims to provide schools with suggestions for planning the content of their progressive programmes in these three activities.

Jim Hall
March 2005

# Gymnastic Activities

# Introduction to Gymnastic Activities

The Gymnastic Activities lesson includes varied floorwork on a clear floor, unimpeded by gymnastic apparatus, chairs, trolleys or a piano, followed by varied apparatus work that covers half to two-thirds of the lesson time. The apparatus will have been placed around the sides and ends of the hall, near to where it will be positioned and used in the lesson.

The focus is on the body and helping each pupil to move neatly with control and versatility. The lessons should also be physically demanding to develop strength and suppleness. Activities include the natural movements of running, jumping, landing, rolling, climbing, swinging, balancing, taking weight onto hands, bending, stretching and twisting. Performing these movements maintains and develops the body's capacity to use them. Traditional, popular gymnastic skills include rolls, handstands, cartwheels, headstands, rope climbing, circling on bars, balances on inverted benches and easy vaults on to and from a low box. Awareness of the variety and contrasts possible in movement and how to demonstrate them can be developed through experiencing different shapes, directions, levels, speeds and amounts of force, which can all be applied to enhance and progress a performance.

The naturalness and variety of what is being taught, children's enthusiasm for movement and their energy and capacity for hard work, and the high standards of performance that the majority can achieve all combine to make Gymnastic Activities lessons a valuable, exciting part of the Physical Education programme.

The following pages provide a scheme of work for Year 2 Gymnastic Activities. There is a lesson plan for each month and an accompanying page of explanatory notes, designed to help teachers and schools with ideas for lessons that are progressive and implement the NC requirements. The lessons usually run for four weeks to allow pupils to practise, repeat, learn, remember and develop the skills involved.

It is hoped that these pages also help to produce a sense of staff-room togetherness regarding the nature of good practice and high standards in teaching Gymnastic Activities lessons. Without this sense of unity among the teachers concerned, there is no continuity of expectations or programme and there will be a less than satisfactory level of achievement.

# Why do we teach Gymnastic Activities?

○ Because it is the most active of all Physical Education activities. It exercises and develops all muscle groups and it stretches and bends all joints to their full range.
**We want our still-growing pupils to grow well.**

○ Because it uses and develops skill in natural activities such as running, jumping, rolling, balancing, climbing, swinging, inverting, bending, stretching, arching and twisting in many challenging situations, on the floor and on apparatus. Self-control and body management are practised and developed, leading to good, confident, poised, controlled, versatile and safe movement in daily life.
**We want our pupils to move well.**

○ Because the actions being practised are natural, improvement can be quick if enthusiastic pupils work hard. A pupil's regard for and attitude towards his or her physical self, particularly at primary school stage, is important to the development of self-image and to the value given to oneself.
**We want our pupils to feel self-confident and pleased with themselves.**

○ Because pupils have to co-operate to share space safely and considerately with others, work together to lift, carry, place and use apparatus, take turns, demonstrate and be demonstrated to, the Gymnastic Activities lesson can develop an enhanced capacity for pleasant, co-operative social relationships.
**We want our pupils to work and get on well with others.**

○ Because Gymnastic Activities provide opportunities for exciting, almost adventurous actions (particularly climbing, swinging, balancing, jumping and landing) and vigorous physical exercise – seldom experienced away from school – these lessons should be seen as antidotes to the increasingly inactive, sedentary and unhealthy lifestyles of many children.
**We want our pupils to be excited by these lessons and use them as outlets for their energy. We want them to believe that exercise is good for you; is good for your heart; and makes you feel and look better.**

# The Gymnastic Activities lesson plan

One answer to the question 'What do we teach in a Gymnastic Activities lesson?' might be 'All the natural actions and ways of moving of which the body is capable and which, if practised whole-heartedly and safely, ensure normal, healthy growth and physical development.'

It has been said that 'What you don't use, you lose.' Most pupils nowadays seldom use their natural capacity for vigorous running, jumping and landing from a height; rolling in different directions; balancing on a variety of body parts; upending to take their weight on their hands; gripping, climbing and swinging on a rope; hanging, swinging and circling on a bar; or whole body bending, stretching, arching and twisting. These natural movements and actions should be present in every Gymnastic Activities lesson, ensuring that pupils do not lose the ability to perform them and have their physical development diminished.

A class teacher's determination to inspire the class to use and not lose their natural physicality can be strengthened by looking at the cars queuing as near to the school exit as possible, ready to transport children home – with the minimum of walking – to their after-school, house-bound, sedentary inaction.

**Floorwork** starts the lesson and includes:

a   activities for the legs, exploring and developing the many actions possible when travelling on foot, and ways to jump and land;

b   activities for the body, including the many ways to bend, stretch, rock, roll, arch, twist, curl and turn, and the many ways in which body parts receive, support and transfer the body weight in travelling and balancing;

c   activities for the arms and shoulders, the least used parts of our body. We strengthen them by using them to hold all or part of the body weight, on-the-spot or moving. This strength is needed in gripping, climbing, hanging, swinging and circling, and in levering on to and across apparatus, supported by the hands only.

**Apparatus work** is the second part of the lesson, making varied, unique and challenging physical demands of pupils whose whole body – legs, arms and shoulders, back and abdominals – has to work strongly because of the more difficult:

○   travelling on hands and feet, over, under, across and around obstacles, as well as vertically, often supported only by the hands

○   jumping and landing from greater heights

○   rolling on to, along, from and across apparatus

○   gripping, swinging, climbing and circling on ropes and bars.

**Final floor activity**, after the apparatus has been returned to its starting places around the sides and ends of the hall, brings the whole class together again in a simple activity based on the lesson's main emphasis. After the bustle of apparatus removal – the swishing of ropes along trackways, the creaking of climbing frames being wheeled away, the bumping down of benches, planks, boxes and trestles – there is a quiet, calm, thoughtful and focused ending to the lesson.

# Apparatus work

Apparatus work is the most important part of the lesson and one of the most exciting areas within the programme. Pupils work, almost non-stop, at natural, popular activities as they run, jump, climb, roll, balance, swing, hang, circle and up-end, taking their weight on their hands. Three unsatisfactory systems are encountered in primary schools:

1   Apparatus is never used as teachers feel insecure and fearful of accidents. Extended floorwork frustrates the pupils who thus behave badly, making the teacher even less willing to use apparatus.

2   Apparatus is brought out at the start of the morning or afternoon, and left in the same place for each class. This system, often put in place by 'apparatus monitors' (the school caretaker or welfare staff) whose apparatus lay-out applies to all classes:

   a   prevents the safe teaching of floorwork and basic skills because the floor is cluttered with apparatus

   b   gives no credit to the intelligence and ability of children, who enjoy and are perfectly capable of handling apparatus

**c** stifles the development of any standards

**d** breaches the NC requirement that pupils should be taught how to lift, carry, place and use equipment safely.

**3** The apparatus is brought out from a store outside the hall, or at one end of the hall, assembled, used and then returned to the remote store, every lesson. This time-consuming system, with pile-ups at doors or at the end of the room, can take up to five minutes of the lesson time, both before and after apparatus work, instead of the minute, or less, needed in the next and recommended system.

The **recommended system** for ensuring that apparatus is lifted, carried and placed in position quickly and easily needs the co-operation of all the teachers. Before lessons start in the morning or afternoon, the portable apparatus is placed around the sides and ends of the hall adjacent to where it will be used. Each group of pupils will thus only have to carry it 2–3 metres. A well-trained class can have the apparatus in place in 30 seconds. Each day, after all lessons are finished, as much of the apparatus as possible should remain in the hall – in corners, against or on the platform, or at the sides and ends of the room. Mats can sometimes be stored vertically behind climbing frames, benches and boxes.

## Organising groups for apparatus work

Because the combinations of apparatus used in infant lessons are usually simple, such as bench and mat, or low box and mat, groups of four pupils are sufficient per piece of apparatus. The organisation of the seven or eight mixed infant groups is done in September. Pupils are told, 'These are your groups and starting places for apparatus work.' For the four- or five-lesson development of a lesson, the same groups go to the same starting places, becoming more expert in lifting, carrying and placing their piece of apparatus.

At the end of the apparatus work, groups return to their starting places to return the apparatus to its original position around the sides and ends of the room. The floor is now clear for the incoming class to start its lesson.

For variety, and to extend their lifting and carrying expertise, groups can be placed at a new set of 'number one apparatus' at the start of the next new lesson.

## Fixed and portable apparatus

Apparatus referred to in the lesson plans that follow, and shown in the examples of simple and larger apparatus groupings, include the following items:

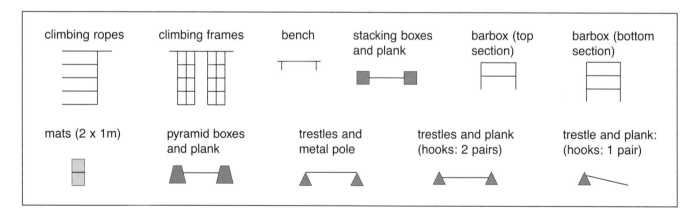

Minimum number recommended:
- ❍ 12 × mats (2 × 1 m)
- ❍ 3 × benches
- ❍ 1 × barbox that can be divided into two smaller boxes by lifting off the top section. The lower section should have a platform top
- ❍ 1 × pair stacking boxes, 19 × 19 in (48 × 48 cm) base, 13 in (33 cm) high; and one 8 ft (2.4 m) plank
- ❍ 1 × pair pyramid boxes, 31 in (78 cm) high, 24 in (60 cm) long, 21 in (53 cm) wide at base tapering to 15 in (38 cm) wide at top, and one 8 ft (2.4 m) plank
- ❍ 1 × pair of 3 ft (1 m), 3.5 ft (1.06 m), 4.6 ft (1.4 m) trestles
- ❍ 2 × planks with two pairs of hooks
- ❍ 2 × planks with one pair of hooks
- ❍ 1 × 10 ft (3 m) metal pole

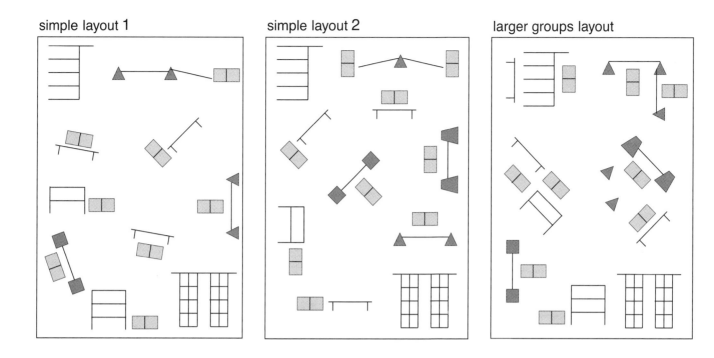

| simple layout 1 | simple layout 2 | larger groups layout |

# Observing a Gymnastic Activities lesson

## The hall

**a** Clean floor?

**b** Satisfactory temperature?

**c** Safe, with no intrusive, dangerous piano, chairs, tables or trolley?

**d** Clear floor sockets for securing bolts of frames and ropes?

## The class

**a** Safely and sensibly dressed – no watches, rings, long sleeves or trousers, unbunched hair, socks without shoes?

**b** Well-behaved – no uninvited talking; instant response to instructions; sharing floor and apparatus unselfishly; attentive, interested observers of demonstrations; sensible and co-operative in lifting, carrying and placing apparatus safely?

## The teacher

**a** Sensibly dressed for a 'physical' lesson, with appropriate footwear, at least, as an example?

**b** Is there a lesson plan as a reminder of the lesson's content?

## The teaching

**a** Is the class 'put in the picture' regarding the lesson's main aim, emphasis or theme?

**b** Are opportunities being provided for planning the activities? 'Can you plan a short sequence of some of your favourite balances?'

**c** Are opportunities being provided for reflecting on and evaluating work observed, or performed by self? 'What three very neat travelling actions did Susan demonstrate?'

**d** Are 'dead spots', when no-one is working, being kept to a minimum? Or are lessons interrupted by:

○ over-long instructions and explanations

○ too many demonstrations and too many, long-winded reflections?

## Apparatus

a   placed around sides and ends of the hall near to where it will be positioned and used?

b   brought out and put away quietly, carefully and sensibly?

## General Impression

a   Is the hall 'a scene of busy activity with everyone being found to be working, not waiting', almost all of the time?

b   Are deep breathing, perspiration and smiling faces evident to prove that pupils are working vigorously and whole-heartedly at a variety of activities, which they are enjoying?

c   Does the lesson have a satisfactory conclusion? Praise? Thanks? Is there a relaxed and calm atmosphere?

# Safe practice and accident prevention

In Physical Education lessons, where one of the main aims is to contribute to healthy growth and development, we must do everything possible to ensure safety and accident prevention.

**Good supervision** by the teacher at all times is a main contributor to safety. The first question asked after a serious injury is always 'Was the teacher with the class?' He or she must be there and teaching in positions from which the majority of the class can be seen. This usually means circulating on the outside looking in, with no-one behind his or her back.

**Good teaching** develops the correct, safe method of landing from a height; taking weight on the hands; gripping apparatus or rolling. The outward expression of the caring attitude we try to create is a sensible, unselfish sharing of hall and apparatus space, and self-control in avoiding others.

**Badly behaved classes** who do not respond immediately, starting or stopping as requested; who rush around selfishly and noisily, disturbing others; who are never quiet in their speech or their body movements; and who do not try to move well, are destructive of any prospect of high standards of safety or lesson enjoyment.

**A safe environment** requires a well-behaved, quiet, attentive and responsive class. Good behaviour must be continually pursued until it becomes the normal, expected way to work in every lesson.

**The hall** should be at a good working temperature, with windows and doors opened or closed as necessary, to cope with changing seasons and room temperatures. Potentially dangerous chairs, piano, tables and trolleys should be removed if possible, or pushed against a wall or into a corner. Floor sockets should be regularly cleared of cleaning substances, which harden and block the small sockets.

**Before the lesson starts** the teacher should check for sensible, safe clothing with no watches, rings or jewellery, which can cause serious scarring and injury, as well as long trousers that can catch heels and unbunched hair that can impede vision.

**Barefoot work is recommended** because it is quiet, provides a safe, strong grip on apparatus, and enhances the appearance of the work. Barefoot work also enables the little used muscles of the feet and ankles to develop as they grip, balance, support, propel and receive the body weight.

# National Curriculum requirements for Gymnastics Activities – Key Stage 1: The Main Features

'The government believes that two hours of physical activity a week, including the National Curriculum for Physical Education and extra-curricular activities, should be an aspiration for all schools. This applies to all stages.'

## Programme of study

*Pupils should be taught to:*

a   perform basic skills in travelling; being still; finding and using space both on the floor and using apparatus
b   develop the range of their skills and actions (for example, balancing, jumping and landing, climbing, rolling)
c   link skills and actions in short movement phrases
d   create and perform short, linked sequences that show a clear beginning, middle and end with contrasts in direction, level and speed.

## Attainment target

*Pupils should be able to demonstrate that they can:*

a   select and use skills, actions and ideas appropriately, applying them with control and co-ordination
b   copy, explore and remember skills, and link them in ways that suit the activities
c   observe and talk about differences between their own and others' performances and use this understanding to improve their own performance.

## Main NC headings when considering assessment of progression and expectation

**Planning** thoughtfully precedes the performance. Pupils think ahead to what their response will be, trying to 'see' the intended outcome. Evidence of satisfactory planning is seen in:

a   sensible, safe judgements
b   an obvious understanding of what was asked for
c   good use of the movement elements that enhance and provide quality, variety and contrast.

**Performing and improving performance** is the main aim and evident as pupils:

a   work hard, concentrating on the main features of the task
b   practise to show safe, skilful, controlled activity
c   demonstrate that they can remember and repeat the actions.

**Linking actions together**, with control, into 'sentences of movement' with a still start and finish and a flowing middle, provides a basis for progression, and is evident as pupils:

a   work harder for longer
b   work more confidently
c   show greater use of the space, shape and effort elements that provide attractive variety and contrast in sequences.

**Reflecting and making judgements** is evident as pupils:

a   describe the most important features of a demonstration
b   suggest ways to improve
c   self-evaluate and act upon their own reflections.

# Year 2 Gymnastic Activities programme

Pupils should be able to:

| Autumn | Spring | Summer |
|---|---|---|
| **1** Respond quickly to instructions, performing whole-heartedly, vigorously and safely. | **1** Show ability and desire to respond safely and quickly to tasks in varied ways. | **1** Respond to set tasks with confidence and enthusiasm. |
| **2** Work, almost non-stop, trying to do neat, quiet performances. | **2** Practise whole-heartedly and continuously, focusing on actions, body parts used and good spacing. | **2** Manage the body in a well-controlled way, using the full range of movement in the joints and muscles concerned. |
| **3** Share floor and apparatus space unselfishly with others. | **3** Balance well on varied parts and show good, firm shapes. | **3** Show good space awareness – knowing how to slow down, speed up, pause to accommodate and not impede others sharing the space. |
| **4** Pursue competence, originality and versatility by thoughtful, well-planned practising. | **4** Be effort and speed aware, feeling good body tension for a controlled performance. | **4** Use varied speeds and effort for more spectacular performances – explosive jumps, gentle rolls, firm balances, slow stretches and curls, strong climbs. |
| **5** In travelling and flight, use vigorous, varied take-off and landing actions, using arms well for balance. | **5** Be body-shape aware in stillness, balance and travelling. | |
| **6** Support body weight on hands safely with straight arms, head forwards, and just the right amount of effort in the push. | **6** Be keen to improve, working hard, alone, and with partner. | **5** Co-operate with a partner, travelling together, copying each other, observing and commenting, and working in unison. |
| **7** Include firm, still balances within sequences as contrast to continuous, vigorous action. | **7** Co-operate with a partner to mirror, contrast, lead, follow. | **6** Show a well-practised expertise in lifting, carrying, placing apparatus, quickly, quietly and safely with others. |
| **8** Be body-shape aware to progress the work and improve its style. | **8** Work, almost non-stop, with no queuing or impeding others. | |
| **9** Be body-parts aware, 'feeling' how the parts are working. | **9** Work hard to deserve praise and stamp work with own special style and personality. | **7** Feel that they have progressed and understand the nature of the progress, e.g. excellent jumps and landings; varied rolls; weight on hands with confidence; smooth rolls; and well-linked sentences. |
| **10** Demonstrate increasing control and understanding by including direction and level changes. | **10** Plan and perform sequences of actions linked neatly, quietly, with control and poise. | |
| **11** Be reminded of the correct, safe way to lift, carry and place apparatus, working with others. | **11** Show ability to approach, mount, travel on and leave apparatus without impeding others, and with interesting, versatile contrasts such as jumps, rolls, balances and inversion. | **8** Approach, mount, travel on and dismount from apparatus, responding to set tasks with confidence and enthusiasm. |
| **12** Link movements with control. | **12** Observe performances with interest and suggest ways in which they might be improved. | **9** Observe demonstrations and comment on actions and any features worth copying or learning from. |
| **13** Observe a performance and comment on what was well done and worth copying. | | **10** Recognise the effects of physical activity on bodies – deep breathing, faster pulse rate, feeling hot, becoming exhausted. |

# Lesson Plan 1 • 30 minutes
### September

**Emphasis on:** *(a) unselfish co-operation in sharing floor and apparatus space; (b) immediate responses to instructions; (c) variety in travelling on floor and apparatus, using feet, feet and hands, and other body surfaces.*

## Floorwork
### 12 minutes

### Legs

1 Can you walk, run, jump and land without stopping, and carry on with your walking again?

2 Because you are travelling non-stop, look ahead and plan to walk, then run just the right distance to let you do your lively jump in a good space.

3 Can you show me other ways to travel, using legs only? (For example, skip, bounce, gallop, hopscotch, slip sideways.)

### Body

1 Lie down on your back, front or side. Stretch your body out fully, reaching your arms above your head and pointing your toes. Can you travel by changing to a curled shape? Try it again. (For example, to lying curled on one side after sideways roll.)

2 From your bent shape, can you now travel to a new supporting part, with your body stretched again? (For example, roll on to knees, stretch arms forwards and up above head.)

3 Now can you do one more curl and stretch for me? (For example, roll to a sitting, curled position, then rock back to stretched shoulder balance.) Go back to your starting position and try again.

### Arms

1 Look for a clear space each time, then travel slowly on hands and feet. Try to show me your actions clearly.

2 Are you sometimes using hands and feet apart, and sometimes closer together? Which way is easier?

3 Can you travel by moving hands only and then feet only, stretching, then curling your body?

## Apparatus Work
### 16 minutes

1 Using feet only, travel to all parts of the room where you see good spaces, but do not touch any apparatus.

2 Can you do your floorwork, walking, running and jumping without stopping? (For example, walking across, under, through, in and out of apparatus; running on floor, across mats, astride benches; jumping over mats, benches, low planks.)

3 Use your feet only to bring you on to, take you along, then bring you off the apparatus. Plan to show me a good variety of actions. (For example, step, jump or bounce on; walk, skip, high jump from.)

4 Now you may use both hands and feet to take you travelling up to, on, along and from the apparatus. Travel slowly enough for me to see your different actions clearly.

5 Earlier, in our floorwork, we travelled by going from a stretch to a curl. Can you now travel on floor and all apparatus, changing from a long, stretched body to one that is curled up small? (For example, up and down the climbing frames; on two ropes with a stretched swing to a curled landing; under and on poles, planks, benches and boxes; rolling across mats.)

## Final Floor Activity
### 2 minutes

Show me one way to travel, using your feet silently.

**Gymnastic Activities**

# Teaching notes and NC guidance
# Development over 4 lessons

## Floorwork

### Legs

1   Pupils will jump, land and be still, if it is not emphasised that we 'land and keep going!'

2   The jump is the main feature, and some pupils will need to be dissuaded from running long distances without a jump.

3   Much teacher commentary on activities observed and selected demonstrations will inspire the variety aimed for in this lesson.

### Body

1   It helps to produce a quick response if the teacher suggests a starting, stretched position from which it is easy to curl up.

2   If the class are slow to respond, once again the teacher can suggest a next move which satisfies the set task.

3   From needing an assisted start to the sequence, the class, week by week, will begin to introduce their own ideas for supporting parts, and even include different levels.

### Arms

1   Insist on 'slow travelling, using both hands and feet. No quick scampering!' Rushing around in and out of one another is common, but puts little weight on hands and does little to build skill, strength or understanding.

2   'Hands and feet apart' can mean a cartwheel, as well as the travel with hands and feet both supporting down near the floor. Wide hands and feet, with a long body near to floor, is difficult to support. Hands and feet close in a high arch is also difficult.

3   You can have front (the usual), back or one side to the floor as you move hands only, then feet only.

## Apparatus Work

1   Travel everywhere, except on apparatus. To test pupils' 'immediate responses' and their 'unselfish sharing of floor', the teacher can call 'Stop!' Praise those who respond immediately and those who are in a space, well away from others.

2   With good planning and thinking ahead, pupils can travel non-stop, walking, running and jumping as appropriate.

3   'Feet only travelling' means that we cannot use ropes, and can only step on and off the climbing frames from a low height. Praise neat, quiet actions with good body shapes and good use of arms for any balancing from jumps.

4   'Hands and feet travelling now' brings all apparatus into use. Discourage queues at favourite ropes and climbing frames, and encourage a continuous circulation from piece to adjacent piece.

5   Revision of the floorwork, plus new work now possible on floor and apparatus, will challenge pupils' planning ability as they climb, roll, swing, circle, vault, travel, while thinking about their changing body shapes. It will also challenge the teacher to be aware of what is going on and to comment on and demonstrate it, if it seems a good addition to the class repertoire.

## Final Floor Activity

The teacher can say 'If I close my eyes and ask you to travel on your feet so silently that I cannot hear you, what action or actions will you choose to use?'

# Lesson Plan 2 • 30 minutes
## October

**Emphasis on:** *(a) controlling the body shape to enhance the appearance of a performance and to make you work harder; (b) observing demonstrations with interest, and describing the actions enjoyed and any special features.*

## Floorwork
### 12 minutes

### Legs

1   Stand tall and still on tiptoes. Run and jump up into a beautifully stretched jump with straight arms high above head. Land softly and show a still, tall finish.

2   Try one- and two-footed take-offs to see which gives you more height and time to make your big stretch in the air.

3   You can land with feet apart, side to side, or one in front of the other. Or you can land with one foot after the other, which slows you down nicely for your neat, still finish. On landing, feel how straight arms help your balance.

### Body

1   Can you keep at least one hand on the floor and show me how to join together different body movements and shapes, such as bending, stretching, twisting and arching?

2   If you are short of ideas, lie on your back with hands on the floor and body wide stretched. Now come up to sitting curled; change to side, falling stretched on one hand and one foot; put the top (non-supporting) hand under the other arm and twist to lie on back again.

3   I will find your linking movements interesting. Show me slowly and clearly how you change from shape to shape.

### Arms

1   With one, both or alternate hands on the floor, can you lift your legs in the air, stretching them long and high?

2   Your arms will also be long and straight for a safe, strong support.

## Apparatus Work
### 16 minutes

1   Run silently in and out of one another without touching any apparatus except mats. When I call 'Stop!' show me a clear, still body shape on the nearest apparatus. 'Stop!'

2   When I stop you next time, try to show me a body shape that contrasts with one of the others on the apparatus with you.

3   Travel up to your first piece of apparatus and arrive on it with your body curled up strongly. (For example, hanging from pole, rope or plank; crouched small on feet on climbing frame or box top; curled on shoulders on mat, plank or box; lying on one side on plank, box or mat.) From this still start, change to travelling on your apparatus and try to include clear body shapes as you go. After you leave the apparatus, show me a still, tall, stretched finishing position.

4   Stay at your number one apparatus and show me a sequence that includes: (a) strong leg and arm travelling actions; (b) varied body movements – bending, stretching, curling, twisting; (c) a variety of clear body shapes, both still and moving; (d) a still starting and finishing position on the floor away from the apparatus.

## Final Floor Activity
### 2 minutes

How many travelling actions can you do with a leg or legs nicely stretched?

# Teaching notes and NC guidance
# Development over 4 lessons

## Floorwork

### Legs

1 Good posture and tall, erect, unsagging carriage are commented on right from the start of the lesson. A whole-hearted effort is needed to produce this clearly stretched, whole-body shape in flight – and whole-heartedness is always one of our aims.

2 Only a short, 3–4 metre run is needed to prepare you for the settle and upwards spring, which is strongest from both feet.

3 A slow, controlled landing is easier if feet land one after the other, slowing you down gradually. Straight arms forwards or sideways act to balance you.

### Body

1 The body movement part of the floorwork is often the most difficult to get started, because the actions and movements are unusual and not often experienced. All the more important, therefore, to encourage these big body movements in order to retain our whole body suppleness and strength.

2 A directed start by the teacher helps the class to understand the task and gives them starting points from which to develop their own ideas during future lessons.

3 All sequences of joined-up movements need linking actions. Skill in linking actions is as admirable and worth praising as good performances of the main movements.

### Arms

1 Ensure that all pupils have good space behind them to let them kick up a leg into their cartwheels or handstands. The kicking-up leg is straight and stays stretched during the move.

2 Straight arms tend to stay unbending and strong. Any 'give' in the arm while up-ended can easily cause a collapse.

## Apparatus Work

1 Encourage running 'in and out of one another' to and from all directions, rather than all following all in one big circle. The 'Stop!' lets the teacher check on the quality of pupils' spacing and their immediate response to a signal.

2 If there are four or five sharing a set of apparatus, the one you choose to contrast with might in turn be concentrating on another. We hope to see a variety of supporting body parts, not always the easy support on feet, or hands and feet.

3 A stationary start on the floor is followed by a travel up to and a stationary, held, curled body position on your first piece of apparatus. Pupils then stay on and travel on the apparatus, trying to emphasise changing body shapes as they go.

4 'Number one apparatus' means the group which a team brought out. Teams should be reasonable in size, and start off by standing on the floor, 3–4 metres away from their apparatus. This starting signal is matched by a similar finishing signal after including all the parts in the challenge. (Groups rotate clockwise and anti-clockwise in alternate lessons, aiming to visit three or four sets of apparatus in any one lesson. All sets of apparatus will be visited at least once per fortnight.)

## Final Floor Activity

Leaping, hurdling, high bouncing, jumping, walking, hopping, hopscotch, slipping sideways.

# Lesson Plan 3 • 30 minutes
## November

**Emphasis on:** *(a) space awareness, and the unselfish sharing and good use of it (directions, levels, own and general space); (b) linking movements with obvious control and understanding.*

## Floorwork
### 12 minutes

### Legs

1 In your own small floor space, can you run with high knee-lifts? Then show me your choice of ways to travel, using legs and covering the whole floor space.

2 In your travelling all around the room, can you plan to follow the same pathway each time?

3 Can you include a direction change somewhere? Don't always travel forwards.

### Body

1 Can you join together three bridge-like shapes, supporting yourself perfectly still each time on different body parts?

2 You can stand, kneel or lie, and your back, front or side can be towards the floor. You might even be up-ended on shoulders.

3 It would be very good to see two or more different levels, please. (For example, high on tiptoes, body angled down; medium crab; low sitting or lying.)

### Arms

1 Can you take your body weight on to one, two or alternate hands, take your legs up into the air space above your head, then bring them down to a different floor space?

2 Handstanders can take legs high into the space. If you are happier doing lower bunny jumps, remember to plan to move your feet to a different finishing place on the floor.

3 Slow and quiet movements will look best. Keep your arm or arms straight for a safe, strong support.

## Apparatus Work
### 16 minutes

1 Touching only the floor and mats to start with, can you show me some running or bouncing in your own floor space; include some neat, travelling actions to take you across, along, around, under, or in and out of the apparatus without touching any?

2 From a still start in a floor space each time, can you plan ways to travel up to, on to, along and from the apparatus with a change of direction somewhere?

3 Touching apparatus with hands only, take your weight onto your hands with straight arms and bent legs. Can you bring your feet down softly in a new floor space?

4 Use all the apparatus as you travel freely about the room. Plan to show me different levels at which you can travel and hold a still position on the apparatus. (For example, travel high on climbing frames; roll low across mats or pull along benches; walk in a medium crab arch; hold a high stand on a box top, a medium arch on a plank, or a low body close to a bench or mat.)

## Final Floor Activity
### 2 minutes

Plan and show me a pattern of movements that includes an action on the spot, followed by movements where you travel forwards, sideways, backwards or diagonally.

## Gymnastic Activities

# Teaching notes and NC guidance
# Development over 4 lessons

## Floorwork

### Legs

1   Work in your own space for about eight running steps, knees high and arms working strongly to balance legs. Then travel about the whole space, planning to make a pathway that you can remember and repeat. For example, an oval, circle, triangle or figure of eight.

2   Because pupils are following the same pathway in the whole room space, they might need to perform their travel action on the spot sometimes if they see a crowd ahead of them, impeding progress.

3   Be very careful if travelling backwards. Look over one shoulder.

### Body

1   Pupils can be asked to identify any bridge-like shapes in the room as a guide to their arched shape making.

2   Demonstrations and teacher commentary on the varied possible supporting parts are necessary to increase the class repertoire. Some of the arches can be very small, such as that below knees while sitting, or below body while on elbows and knees.

3   Changing levels requires good linking movements – sitting, twisting, lowering, springing, rolling, rocking, tilting.

### Arms

1   Ask class to look at a mark on the floor where they are standing at the start. Their next takeoff spot will be from a new mark.

2   Pupils can pretend to be taking weight on hands on a low box top, and coming down on the opposite side, by twisting hips and legs against the fixed hands.

3   'Slow' gives the impression of everything being under control. A still, erect starting and finishing position also enhances the appearance of the work.

## Apparatus Work

1   A repeat of the starting leg activity, but with the need to plan ahead to negotiate apparatus.

2   Sideways travel on most apparatus is easy, particularly if moving on hands and feet. A jump up sideways from bench, low box or planks is done carefully and only when there is plenty of space.

3   The teacher can say 'Show me your hands and straight arms' as class hold arms forwards. Fingers should be spread and to the front, with arms in the strong, straight and safe position they will use. Short-lever, bent legs lift up more quickly than legs kept straight. On some apparatus, hands are flat on top. On others, they grip the sides. On ropes, hands are close together, gripping. On climbing frames, one hand will be gripping a bar higher than the other hand.

4   The message is probably 'on and hold; travel and hold; travel and off. Travel to next piece of apparatus.' During demonstrations the observers can be asked to 'look out for and tell me about good, held positions and their levels. Look out for and tell me about interesting travelling you see at different levels.'

## Final Floor Activity

This could be as simple as a group of four jumps on the spot, alternating with jumping or travelling forwards a short distance for four, then to one side for four, then back to starting place for four.

# Year 2

# Lesson Plan 4 • 30 minutes
## December

**Emphasis on:** *(a) jumping strongly and landing softly, absorbing shock; (b) rolling; (c) participating whole-heartedly in almost non-stop physical activity.*

## Floorwork
### 12 minutes

### Legs

1 Do little jumps on the spot, stretching ankles strongly to push you. Keep your body straight, but let your knees bend to make the landings soft and quiet. Jump, land, bend.

2 After a short run of about four strides, jump straight up, pushing up with one or both feet. Stretch body again in the air. Do a soft, squashy landing, with a good knee bend.

3 Now swing both arms high above head to help your jump. When you land, show me how your arms stretched forwards or sideways can help your balanced, controlled landings.

### Body

1 Lie on your back, curled up small, then roll backwards and forwards from seat all the way to your shoulders and hands. Put your chin on your chest to keep your back rounded.

2 Now lie on your back, curled up small, with hands clasped under knees. Roll from side to side. Try to roll to one side, then the other side, then right over on to your back again. 'Side to side... and right over.'

3 Lie on your back with body straight and arms by your sides. Keep straight and roll over on to your front, then on to your back again. Pull across with the opposite shoulder or straight leg.

### Arms

1 Put both hands on the floor with arms straight and fingers pointing forwards. Now jump your feet off the floor, gradually bouncing up higher.

2 Keep your head looking forwards. If you look back under your arms, everything will be upside down.

3 Try three or four preparatory jumps. When you feel ready, give an extra strong push to take your shoulders above your hips and your hips above your hands.

## Apparatus Work
### 16 minutes

1 Walk around the room, touching floor and mats only. You may run and jump on to or across mats, benches and low planks.

2 When you land from your jump, try a squashy landing and a full knee bend that takes you right down on to your back. Finish by rolling sideways, spring up on to feet, and off you go again!

3 Now step up on to apparatus. Jump off, keeping your body nicely stretched, and do a soft, quiet, squashy landing. If you like, add in a sideways roll again, then off to the next apparatus.

4 Can you use a bunny-jump action to bring you on to a piece of apparatus? Hands grip sides or are flat on top, then jump and pull or twist feet up on to apparatus. Leave with either a jump, or a roll off from a sitting, kneeling or lying position.

## Final Floor Activity
### 2 minutes

To a four-count beat, can you make up a simple pattern of jumping in your own floor space? (For example, one foot to same; one foot to other; one foot to both; both feet to both.)

*Gymnastic Activities*

# Teaching notes and NC guidance
# Development over 4 lessons

## Floorwork

### Legs

1 At the start, talk about and look at good ankle actions. Because the ankle joint is seldom fully extended in everyday life, there will be many poor performances. The feeling is of the head pushing up and the toes pushing and pointing down.

2 Emphasise 'upwards jump, not long jump' as pupils go higher because of the run up. Ankle and knee joints 'give' slowly on landing, to absorb shock and keep it quiet.

3 Good arm action helps the lift-off, the balance in the air, the balance on landing, and the appearance of the performance.

### Body

1 We are used to travelling on feet, and on feet and hands, but not so used to travelling on other large body parts and surfaces. This long, slow rock from seat all the way to shoulders, with hands next to shoulders and thumbs in, needs to be practised and experienced. The move backwards is like the start of a backward roll. The move forwards is like the end of a forward roll.

2 Those who do not like rolling backwards and forwards do not usually mind the quite long travel of a sideways roll.

3 The straight-body sideways roll is a good rolling activity and a useful way to link two balances together.

### Arms

1 For the little bounces up and down, hands are placed shoulder width apart under the shoulders, with feet and knees together.

2 Head is tilted back a little way to look ahead of where your hands are.

3 Legs are kept well bent to shorten the lever. There will be several examples of well-controlled performances in most classes. Use these to demonstrate.

## Apparatus Work

1 Short runs, with the emphasis on height in the jumping when there is plenty of space and pupils are completely unimpeded.

2 With nine or ten mats available in a typical infant lesson, there will be continuous opportunities for the 'run, jump, squashy landing and roll sideways'.

3 A quick on to, up and from the apparatus, to practise landing from a greater height, with or without the sideways roll.

4 All pieces of apparatus can be arrived on by taking all the weight momentarily on the hands and doing the bunny-jump action. Pupils then travel to a point where it is possible to leave the apparatus either by a jump and a quiet landing, or by a roll.

## Final Floor Activity

'Pattern' means a repeated series of actions. At least two actions are needed to make a series.

# Year 2

# Lesson Plan 5 • 30 minutes
### January

**Emphasis on:** *(a) sequences and linking a series of actions, and showing the ability to remember and repeat them; (b) observing performances with interest, and making comments on what was done and what was liked.*

## Floorwork
### 12 minutes

### Legs

**1** Can you do an upwards jump where you are, then show me a very short run into another high jump?

**2** When you are in the air, can you stretch out your body from straight arms above head down to pointed ankles and toes?

**3** Be still for your start and after your finish each time. Always look for a good space to run into.

### Body

**1** Show me a favourite, still body shape (e.g. stretched long or wide, curled, arched, twisted). Can you move on to a different body part and show me a new body shape?

**2** Make up a sequence that you can remember of three or four joined-up and changing body shapes on different body parts.

**3** The linking movements will be particularly interesting to me. I will be looking for any new ideas that I can learn from (e.g. rolls, jumps, twists, lowering, rocking).

### Arms

**1** All start ready in a crouch position, as for a bunny jump. Show me a pattern of ways you like to travel using hands and feet. Show me contrasting actions.

**2** Variety can include hands only, then feet only; walk hands, then jump feet forwards; low crawl, then high cartwheel; hands and feet wide, then close together as you travel.

**3** Different body parts can lead the movements and your body can have back, front or one side towards the floor.

## Apparatus Work
### 16 minutes

**1** Show me a beautifully stretched body, standing tall on tiptoes in your own floor space. Jump on the spot, then travel up to and on to a piece of apparatus and show me a still body shape. Leave the apparatus and stop in a new floor space, nicely stretched again.

**2** Start in a space near apparatus. Make your hands important in travelling up to and on to your apparatus. On the apparatus, travel using hands, or hands and feet strongly. See if some of your floorwork travelling can be used. Leave with a high jump and a nice, 'giving' landing, followed by a sideways roll if you want.

**3** Starting at your number one apparatus places, try to do the following sequence for me: (a) start on the floor in your own space, do an upwards jump on the spot, then travel up to and on to the apparatus; (b) show me a firm, still body shape as soon as you arrive on your apparatus, then travel using hands, or hands and feet strongly; (c) just before leaving the apparatus, can you show me a still body shape, different from your first one; (d) leave with a stretched upwards jump or by rolling from the apparatus, and finish, still, in your own floor space.

## Final Floor Activity
### 2 minutes

Show me a starting position with a firm, whole-body shape. Run and jump, making that shape in the air. Change your starting shape and your shape in the air.

# Teaching notes and NC guidance
# Development over 4 lessons

## Floorwork

### Legs

1 Three actions to be linked together. Jump, run and jump. The 'very short' run, of about 3 or 4 metres only, takes you into the space you decided on during your jump on the spot.

2 Twice, in the stationary and running jumps, there is an emphasis on stretching the whole body firmly to make it work as hard as possible and the actions look as good as possible.

3 Infants like to be moving all the time and need to be encouraged to hold still at start and finish.

### Body

1 Arms, legs and spine work together to make the whole-body shapes. The class should be showing shapes while standing, lying, kneeling, sitting, up-ended on shoulders, arched on back or front.

2 Different body shapes on different body parts, all smoothly joined up, will be done in your own space with minimum travelling.

3 Observers can be asked to 'watch the demonstrations carefully and tell me which group of shapes you like. Tell me also how the performer linked the shapes together.'

### Arms

1 Insist on slow, careful travelling, using actions that involve the whole body and put most of the weight on the hands.

2 Ask pupils to put a name to their actions, to make them think about the nature of them. (For example, crawling, hands and feet moving together; stretching out and curling in as hands only go forwards, then feet catch up; bunny jumping forwards from feet to hands, then jump feet up to hands again; bouncing on all fours as long body springs up and down, moving forwards; cartwheels.)

3 We usually travel with head leading and front of body towards the floor.

## Apparatus Work

1 We are trying to encourage pupils to make a short sequence with a beginning, middle and end. This middle is simple and short – make a still body shape after arriving on the apparatus.

2 Varied travelling on hands and feet is still fresh in our memories from the floorwork. Now we practise and develop it on both floor and on apparatus, still looking for variety in actions and leading parts, and whole-body involvement.

3 If groups start at their number one apparatus places, i.e. by the piece of apparatus they brought out, the numbers will be evenly shared around all pieces. On alternate weeks pupils move around clockwise and anti-clockwise, meeting at least three sets of apparatus each lesson. The eventual demonstrations will be of whole groups showing how well they share the apparatus and floor to work almost non-stop at their sequences. They include all the elements from the training in the floorwork, here expanded and developed on floor and apparatus.

## Final Floor Activity

A triangle of three actions to bring you back to your starting place is recommended.

**Year 2**

# Lesson Plan 6 • 30 minutes
### February

**Emphasis on:** *(a) balancing; (b) maintaining good body tension and posture.*

## Floorwork
### 12 minutes

### Legs

1 Stand tall, balanced on tiptoes. Run, jump and land in a beautifully balanced position where your body is supported on one or both legs in a way that is hard to hold steady.

2 Go into your balanced finish slowly so that it becomes a landing changing into a balance, almost in slow motion.

3 The difficulty comes from being on an unusual part of one or both feet, or holding your body in a difficult position.

### Body

1 Choose some part or parts of your body other than feet to balance on. Stretch those parts not being used for support to enhance the look of the balance.

2 From your first balance, can you change to a new supporting part or parts by way of a simple linking movement (such as a roll, twist, spin, arch), still not on feet?

3 Please show me your three balances nicely linked together with an interesting set of supporting parts and linking movements.

### Arms

1 Swing up on to your hands and try to hold a balance for two or three seconds. Make it a strong, safe position by keeping your arms straight and your head looking forwards.

2 Try to let your swinging-up leg go a long way past your head, while the kicking foot hardly leaves the floor. A long, straight line in your legs will help to balance you.

3 'Feel' how much or how little effort is needed to take you up on to your hands. Practise and your body will remember.

## Apparatus Work
### 16 minutes

1 As you visit each piece of apparatus, can you start off standing tall and still? Travel up to and on to the apparatus, and hold a still balance on any body part or parts. Spring up and off your apparatus with a beautifully stretched body in the air. Land in a nicely balanced position with a strong, firm body.

2 Still move from apparatus to apparatus, but this time stay longer on each piece to include travelling actions that can link up balances on different parts of the body and apparatus. Balance, travel; balance, travel; balance, travel; then spring high up and off your apparatus to land, neatly balanced.

3 Starting at your number one places, can you stay and practise to repeat, improve and remember the following: (a) start and finish on the floor in a firm, still, well-balanced position; (b) travel up to, on to, and on your apparatus, including a variety of balances on different body and apparatus parts; (c) leave apparatus with a lively spring and a well-balanced landing; and (d) have one more practice at the handstand just before your finish position.

## Final Floor Activity
### 2 minutes

Show me the hardest balance on one or both feet that you can do without wobbling.

**Gymnastic Activities**

# Teaching notes and NC guidance
# Development over 4 lessons

## Floorwork

### Legs

1 The starting position must be a challenge to hold steady right up on tiptoes. After landing, pupils either hold a position with knees slightly bent, on tiptoes, or they move to standing on one foot, the upper body or other leg in a position that makes balancing difficult.

2 If you rush into a balance, you will almost certainly fail.

3 Near-horizontal standing on one foot, with whole body and other leg inclined forwards or to one side. Upstretched arms add to the difficulty and body tension, and improve the appearance.

### Body

1 Pupils can use any body part or parts as long as there is a problem with being still. The problem is increased by the need to hold non-supporting parts stretched and firm.

2 Pupils have to plan how to move slowly to an adjacent body part to arrive in a new balance. Teacher commentary and many demonstrations will extend class repertoire of such difficult linking movements.

3 Three is sufficiently challenging, but also short enough to be remembered, practised, repeated and improved.

### Arms

1 Long arms swinging from above head, or a short swing up of one leg behind you, are two controlled ways to take you on to your hands.

2 A comparison with a tightrope walker's long, straight pole is recommended to encourage a long line through both legs.

3 We are trying to develop body tension and the feeling of how much effort to apply.

## Apparatus Work

1 We start off with a short, simple sequence, emphasising good, firm body tension throughout. Show a still balance at start and finish, one balance only on the apparatus, and a good move into a balance after a landing from the apparatus.

2 As in the balancing sequence in floorwork, pupils are now moving from balance to balance on apparatus, using travelling actions as linking movements.

3 Over the four weeks of the lesson's development, the class will build up their repertoire, step by step, enabling them to include all the elements within the challenge they have been given. They should experience the variety of working on three different pieces of apparatus each lesson.

## Final Floor Activity

Some will make balancing difficult by working on one foot and placing the other leg in most unusual positions. Others, working on one leg, will use the whole of the upper body, placing it in such difficult positions as tilted horizontally, from upstretched arms right down to stretched, non-supporting leg.

## Year 2 · Lesson Plan 7 · 30 minutes
### March

**Emphasis on:** *(a) partner work, with its enjoyable and co-operative experiences; (b) working hard to achieve success.*

## Floorwork
### 12 minutes

### Legs

1 One partner practises and improves a simple, repeating floor pattern of walking, running, jumping or skipping in own floor space. The other partner practises a repeating pattern, using the whole floor space.

2 One after the other, show your sequence twice through to your partner, who watches and remembers it.

3 Can you now perform together, doing the on-the-spot pattern, then the sequence that uses the whole floor space?

### Body

1 From the same starting position, facing each other, can you very slowly build up a pattern of whole-body movements, taking turns to decide the next one. I am looking for big body stretches (long and wide), curls, twists, arching.

2 Remember to work slowly so that you can mirror each other. Do two, then repeat. Improve and remember them before going on to a third movement.

3 Are you showing any variety (e.g. changing direction or level) or contrast (e.g. a sudden change of speed)?

### Arms

1 Follow your leader, travelling slowly on hands and feet, repeating your pattern of three or four varied actions.

2 Leader, can you include a change of direction, not always travelling forwards?

3 Other partner, you become the new leader now. Keep working at the same sequence. Can you change it slightly by making a different body part lead (e.g. not always the head)?

## Apparatus Work
### 16 minutes

1 One leading, one following, travel up to and on to each group of apparatus, then return to your starting place. Start again with the other partner leading, to see if he or she can remember exactly where you went and what you did.

2 This time, as you follow each other on the apparatus, try to show me good support on hands and feet, with some interesting, big body movements like you used together in the floorwork.

3 Starting on the floor on opposite sides of your piece of apparatus, can you try the following: (a) in own space, partner A demonstrates the leg activity pattern from the start of the floorwork; (b) partner B copies, then travels up to the apparatus, using one or more of the leg actions from the floorwork; (c) partner A copies the travel up to the apparatus; (d) slowly, agreeing who is leader, they pass each other, with an identical action; and (e) travel freely to finish in partner's starting position.

## Final Floor Activity
### 2 minutes

Partner A leads a simple pattern of travelling along straight lines. Partner B leads a pattern of travelling along curving lines.

# Teaching notes and NC guidance
# Development over 4 lessons

## Floorwork

### Legs

1  They must be simple patterns, because they are to be remembered and performed, one after the other. However, to justify the name 'pattern', there must be at least two repeated actions.

2  Each watches the other, once or twice through, then they perform one after the other, starting and finishing side by side.

3  Now they 'follow the leader', facing each other for the routine on the spot, then travelling, one behind the other, using the whole room space.

### Body

1  One partner leads the sequence by showing the first body action. (For example, standing with arms and legs wide, like a star.) Other partner, now in the same wide stance, leads into the second movement. (For example, lower to sitting, curled tight, head on chest.) And so on, slowly, with much repetition of first position.

2  You 'improve' by applying firm body tension to make the whole body shape look neat and under control. No slouching!

3  For example, from the curled sitting pupils could lie down and roll sideways with a stretched body on to front. A sudden change of speed can happen at the very end of a stretch or curl.

### Arms

1  If the pair have their own little 'stage' to work on, not impeding others' floor space, a pattern of three or four ways to travel might take them in a triangle or rectangle back to own starting places.

2  A change of direction happens when your side or your back is leading the travelling, rather than the more usual forward-facing head.

3  Bunny jumps, for example, can be used to travel sideways, with feet and hands zig-zagging along.

## Apparatus Work

1  If the travelling is kept really simple, the whole sequence can take place in instant unison, about 2 metres apart. Follower notes: What actions? How are body parts being used? What shapes are clear within the travelling? Are there any direction changes?

2  The same activity, but with a longer stay on apparatus, giving time for examples of big stretching (wide and long), curling, twisting or arching movements within your travelling.

3  Groups start at their number one apparatus places where they practise, improve and remember all the parts of their sequence. By providing good demonstrations, groups will be helped with ideas for their next piece of apparatus.

## Final Floor Activity

Keep it simple enough to enable the follower to mirror the leader throughout. They change roles when the first leader stops and does an about-turn as a signal to change over duties.

# Lesson Plan 8 • 30 minutes
## April

**Emphasis on:** *(a) awareness and good use of effort and speed to achieve a controlled performance – 'feeling' how we move; (b) using contrasting movements for a more spectacular and polished performance.*

## Floorwork
### 12 minutes

### Legs

1 Travel in a variety of ways, using legs. Can you include actions that are small, light and gentle, and actions that are large, lively and strong?

2 One way to organise it is to do the gentle actions in your own floor space, then the vigorous actions travelling away from and back to your own space.

3 Think about your actions and the ways that the feet and legs are working to make the actions 'feel' so different.

### Body

1 Show me a firm balance and work hard to show a clear body shape. Being balanced means that your body has to work hard not to wobble about.

2 Contrast this strong position by relaxing and gently moving to another part or parts of the body to balance strongly again. Work your body hard to show a firm, clear shape.

3 Be strong, then relax, two or three times, as you plan your sequence of firm balances and contrasting linking actions.

### Arms

1 Travel using straight arms and legs slowly and strongly, with a lot of the weight on your hands.

2 On all fours, can you experiment with hands and feet wide apart, then close together. Which is more difficult?

3 From a standing start, pretend you are travelling side to side along a bench, gripping it with hands only. Let your soft landings contrast with the strong gripping and twisting.

## Apparatus Work
### 16 minutes

1 Travel freely all around the room, showing me easy, quiet leg actions that contrast with a strong, upwards jump on to a mat. Gentle, firm. Easy, strong. Soft, explosive.

2 Travel freely on all the apparatus. Can you contrast for me strong, firm balances, using your whole body well, and your easier travelling actions in between? Coming off, can you do a vigorous upwards jump, then a soft, 'giving' landing and gentle roll?

3 Start at your number one apparatus places to practise, repeat, improve and remember the following: (a) start and finish on the floor, away from the apparatus; (b) as you travel up to and away from the apparatus, include a change of speed at some point (e.g. an explosive jump away from the apparatus at the end of the sequence); (c) alternate travelling and balancing on the apparatus, showing strong balances and some strong travelling with arms straight.

## Final Floor Activity
### 2 minutes

Stand still but relaxed. Accelerate into an explosive, upwards jump with an easy, gentle, quiet landing. Stand tall and relaxed. Repeat.

# Teaching notes and NC guidance
# Development over 4 lessons

## Floorwork

### Legs

1   Gentle, quiet, easy, small steps, skips and bounces. Vigorous, strong, bigger, louder galloping, running and jumping. Run with knees raising high, big bounces and long leaps from foot to foot.

2   A focus on 'where' by everyone will lead to better sharing of the floor in this space-consuming activity. They might even develop a little rhythm. On the spot, 3, 4, 5, 6; travelling for 1... and 2... and 3... and 4... and 5... and home again!

3   To be able to demonstrate ('Who will volunteer?'), pupils must know their actions and uses of the relevant body parts.

### Body

1   Ensure that pupils are balancing with difficulty and not just standing, kneeling or sitting easily.

2   From 'feeling strong' in their firm balance, ask them to feel relaxed and easy as they transfer to another supporting body part, then firm up strongly again.

3   An obvious contrast is in the use of levels, from highest position on tiptoes or one foot, down to being on one knee and one elbow, for example.

### Arms

1   On all fours, walking action; hands only, then feet only; front or back towards floor; hands walk, feet jump to astride hands; or cartwheels.

2   Wide is difficult because arms are at an angle. Close is difficult because you need to be supple enough to bring feet near to hands, arching high.

3   All weight on hands will happen more often now, e.g. for the vertical or lower than vertical cartwheels, or the swing of legs across while staying on hands.

## Apparatus Work

1   The quiet, easy actions will be slower than the accelerating sprint into the dynamic jump.

2   On the apparatus, strong, still balances will alternate two or three times with travelling. At any one time, the hall should be full of still, strong, firm balances and travelling. If necessary, to reinforce the inclusion of balances, the teacher can call out 'Be still, those who are now balancing. The others, keep on travelling, and now... stop! Balancers, start your turn to travel now, keep going... and stop!'

3   All the elements from the floorwork are now being asked for on both floor and apparatus. There will be contrasts of speed and effort, and different 'feelings' within the bodies of the performers at the different parts of their sequences.

## Final Floor Activity

As pupils stand still and tall, their weight is slightly forwards on the balls of the feet, ready for the off. From stillness, they burst into acceleration for the jump, with its explosive drive up and off. A quiet landing nearly in slow motion, with knees and ankles 'giving' and often one foot landing after the other, provides contrasting leg activity.

# Lesson Plan 9 • 30 minutes
## May

**Emphasis on:** *(a) sequences and working harder for longer; (b) responding to set tasks with enthusiasm and confidence.*

## Floorwork
### 12 minutes

### Legs

1 Using your legs, show me a triangle of movements, starting and finishing at the same place. Can you include three different actions and be aware of your body shapes?

2 Variety will come from your different actions and directions. Contrast can come from a change of speed or effort at some point. (An easy, slow, gentle action contrasts with a vigorous, accelerating one.)

3 Legs can travel down at floor level, and lift up higher in shapes like a hurdler, star, tuck, jack-knife, or a mixture (e.g. one leg straight down, the other bent back).

### Body

1 Practise backward, forward and side-to-side rolls from a curled-up sitting position. When you go backwards and forwards, put your hands next to your shoulders and push forwards with them. Side to side, keep hands clasped under knees.

2 Try to roll to one side, to other side, to first side and right over on to your back again. Side, side, side and over.

3 Lie on your back with arms by your side. Twist by lifting one shoulder or leg to take you into a sideways roll, on to front and on to back again.

4 Now, you choose. Start from a low crouch position; or sitting curled; or lying stretched, and plan a roll sequence to include at least two of the three we have practised.

### Arms

1 Slowly and quietly, show me two or more ways to travel on hands, or hands and feet, and see if you could give each action a name, as an introduction, if I asked you to demonstrate.

2 Work in your own small floor space, and show me a still position to signal start and finish each time.

3 Variety will come from a good mixture, such as high on hands, walking or cartwheeling; medium on strong, straight arms and legs, sometimes legs only, sometimes arms only; and low, crouched bunny-jump actions on hands, with bent legs doing a variety of movements.

## Apparatus Work
### 16 minutes

1 Visit each set of apparatus in turn and show me a different method of travelling up to and on to each one for a very short time. Then travel away to a new floor space for your next, different travel.

2 Continue to travel to the apparatus in different ways, but this time take all the weight on your hands to bring you on to the apparatus. A strong bunny-jump grip and action should work at most pieces. Leave with a high jump, a squashy landing and, if there is space on your mat, try a roll.

3 Starting at your number one apparatus places, can you practise, repeat, improve and remember a short sequence of your favourite activities on that apparatus and surrounding floor space?

## Final Floor Activity
### 2 minutes

In a running sequence, can you include changes of direction, body shape and speed?

# Teaching notes and NC guidance
# Development over 4 lessons

## Floorwork

### Legs

1   Ask the class to walk around their little triangle with its 3-metre sides, starting and finishing on the same mark, line, floorboard (or whatever) each time. Walking might even be one of their three different actions.

2   'Different actions' infers greatly differing uses of feet and legs. (For example, easy passing each other as in walking; vigorous running into a leap; hopscotch; mixture of actions.)

3   Asking for 'low, middling and higher feet and leg actions' should inspire some varied ideas worth demonstrating.

### Body

1   The 'hands beside shoulders, thumbs in and fingers spread' is an important teaching point. In a backward roll, hands at shoulders push you on to feet. In a forward roll, hands push you forwards and up on to feet.

2   In rolling sideways, a swing into the movement by the combined knees and clasped hands is essential for a lively action.

3   Left shoulder or leg does the twisting pull to the right.

4   For example, from a low crouch, lower to sitting, and rock backwards and forwards; roll side to side and over on to back; stretch out straight lying on back; roll to left, then to right; sit up curled, rock back on to shoulders and hands; push forwards strongly up on to feet and back to starting crouch position.

### Arms

1   For example, 'I am crawling with straight arms and legs; then walking hands only forwards, and jumping feet up to hands; then I finish with a cartwheel.'

2   If you are kicking feet up to go on to hands, always check that you have room behind you, away from others or apparatus.

3   Like direction changes, level changes provide an obvious and interesting contrast within a performance.

## Apparatus Work

1   The 'up to and away from' travelling is the main emphasis. The two different methods of travel can use feet, or feet and hands.

2   'Feel strong in your hands and arms as you lift, pull, twist, roll, lever, spring' on to apparatus. For variety there should be a strong leg action into the upwards jump and landing, and an easy, slow roll on a mat.

3   During this relatively free activity, the teacher will be able to assess how well the class work on and share the floor and apparatus space; how confident and competent they are in managing their bodies in a wide range of apparatus situations; and how enthusiastically and whole-heartedly they participate in their vigorous physical activity.

## Final Floor Activity

Changing speed in their running will include running on the spot when their progress is impeded by others, plus slowing down and speeding up. Go backwards with great care, looking over one shoulder.

# Lesson Plan 10 • 30 minutes
### June

**Emphasis on:** *(a) partner work to provide enjoyable new learning and social experiences not possible on one's own; (b) extending movement understanding because you need to recognise your partner's movements and be able to repeat your own.*

## Floorwork
### 12 minutes

### Legs

1  Travel side by side or follow the leader, going from space to space. Plan and agree the three varied actions you will use, i.e. one easy and quiet, one with a direction change, and one that explodes into a vigorous movement.

2  Start and finish standing still. After your third movement, go again when you see a big enough space for two of you.

3  A mixture of leading and following, and side by side, would be very interesting (e.g. side by side, going sideways).

### Body

1  Start off, not on your feet, and curl up very small. Stretch part of your body to reach out into the space around you. Curl in tight to support yourself on a new body part.

2  Stretch a different part of your body to a different place in the surrounding space. Curl in tight to your first supporting body part.

3  Show each other your curls and stretches. Plan a way to perform them together, with some contact between you on the two stretches. (Partners will need to adjust their starting positions and relationships to accommodate the stretches.)

### Arms

1  Partner A demonstrates a favourite way to travel on feet and hands, or to be supported on hands only. Partner B observes.

2  Partner B repeats this first action, and adds on one of his or her favourites. Partner A watches.

3  Partner A repeats the two actions, and adds on a third one. Partner B watches carefully.

4  Partner B performs all three actions only or adds in a fourth and last action, with partner A's approval.

## Apparatus Work
### 16 minutes

1  Follow your leader, who travels a short distance on floor and apparatus then stops, to let you copy and catch up. I would like to see some of the varied actions we did on the floor earlier.

2  On apparatus, I would like to see the new leader demonstrating ways to go from a tight curl to a full stretch with a body part reaching out into space. Partner, once again, will observe, then copy. Travel freely, from apparatus to apparatus.

3  Starting at your number one apparatus places, plan and practise: (a) a still starting position on the floor, one behind the other; (b) follow the leader, travelling up to and on to apparatus, using hands strongly to support you, then hold a tight curled position next to each other. New leader takes over, leads slowly into a full stretch, and then travels on apparatus, using hands and feet; (c) same leader comes away from apparatus, using a different leg action from the one that took you on at start.

## Final Floor Activity
### 2 minutes

Take it in turns to be leader. Jump on the spot, then run and jump to face a new direction.

# Teaching notes and NC guidance
# Development over 4 lessons

## Floorwork

### Legs

1 Travelling on a diagonal, one slightly behind the other, takes little space, and still lets one observe the other. Recommend all travel in a straight line, not anti-clockwise in a big circle, getting in one another's way, as so often happens in primary schools.

2 'Your movement is like a sentence, with a start and a finish each time, please.' (A 'sentence' of three words.)

3 Pupils can be very creative and include: one working on the spot, one circling; or parting and closing as they travel.

### Body

1 In the 'stretching and curling sequence', the stretching parts are varied and reach out into different places in space. (Can be to front, side, rear, low, high.) To enable this, we change our starting positions.

2 They can be asked to 'feel' strong and firm as they stretch out the whole body. (No sagging!) Then they 'feel' relaxed and gentle as they fold in to their contrasting curl.

3 Partners can be back to back; side by side; side to back; or facing, as necessary, to permit the momentary contact in the stretches.

### Arms

1 'One favourite way only' must be emphasised, and we want the new activity to be within the capability of the observer.

2 The second action needs to be able to flow on from the first, without too much of a linking problem.

3 As well as being easily linked, we want the next action to have something different about it to maintain the performers' and (later) observers' interest. 'Different' may be the change of level, direction, body shape, body part leading or towards floor, and, of course, actions.

4 The three or four activities, all flowing one after the other, should take three or four lessons to decide and develop.

## Apparatus Work

1 Leader goes and stops while partner observes the actions and any changes of direction, shape or speed. Following partner catches up with leader and stops. Leader, alone, goes and stops.

2 If space permits on a piece of apparatus, include two or three examples of curling, then stretching. On mats, this can include rolls into kneeling, lying or standing stretched. On mats, benches, planks or low box top, the curl can be crouched on two feet, lying on back, front or one side, on knees, up-ended on shoulder and hands. Follow these with the many possible stretchings out.

3 The various floorwork activities are now requested, this time to be performed on floor and apparatus. Include: (a) two ways to travel between apparatus and starting/finishing place on floor; (b) taking whole body weight on hands, and travelling using hands and feet; (c) curling and stretching; (d) observing, copying and working in unison with a partner.

## Final Floor Activity

On the 'jump to face a new direction', partners can arrange to change over their roles as leader and follower.

# Lesson Plan 11 • 30 minutes
### July

**Emphasis on:** *(a) planning activities safely, and performing them with control; (b) practising whole-heartedly to improve, alone and with others; (c) reflecting and commenting on what they and others have done.*

## Floorwork
### 12 minutes

### Legs

1 Rise up on tiptoes with arms nicely stretched sideways for balance. Walk, then run a short distance to jump high and land facing a new direction. Let arms help balance.

2 Each time, look for a clear space, and plan where you will go for your next jump. Never disturb others in the room.

3 Changing direction is helped in the air if you swing into your jump with a strong arm or leg action. Or you can change direction on or after landing.

### Body

1 Make a bridge-like shape, standing with feet apart, body arched forwards, arms angled to the floor. Show me that you can make a different body shape. (For example, feet together, bend legs and back to go down to a curled shape.)

2 Can you now change to a new bridge-like shape? (For example, sitting with bridge below knees.)

3 In your own space, continue to change from a bridge to another shape, back to a bridge, then to another shape. A sequence of three of each would be pleasing.

### Arms

1 Show a partner your best way to take your body weight onto your hands. Your partner will watch, then tell you what he or she particularly liked about your demonstration.

2 Change over. Now the other partner shows a favourite way to take all the weight on to the hands. Once again, the watcher tells what was liked in the demonstration.

3 You might like the neat, still, starting and finishing position; the good, safe, straight arms; the neat body shape, maybe with legs straight and together; or the nice high hips in a bunny jump. Say what you liked.

## Apparatus Work
### 16 minutes

1 Follow your partner, who will take you up to each piece of apparatus, show you a way to take weight onto hands only on the apparatus, then move on to the next place. On and off quickly.

2 Other partner now leads, and shows a short walk, a short run and a careful jump to land on a mat or to cross mat, bench, low plank or low box top. When you land you can try a squashy landing and a roll if you like. Following partner stays back, watching, until there is space to follow and copy.

3 On your own now, start at your number one apparatus places to practise, repeat, improve and remember: (a) a still start and finish on the floor, away from apparatus; (b) travelling on to apparatus, using your arms strongly as you move along or support yourself; (c) within your travelling to see how often you can make a bridge-like shape on apparatus, or on apparatus and adjacent floor.

## Final Floor Activity
### 2 minutes

Stand, balanced, on one or parts of both feet, with arms stretched. Walk a few steps and stop in a different balance on one or both feet.

# Teaching notes and NC guidance
## Development over 4 lessons

## Floorwork

### Legs

1 This activity needs a lot of whole-body control and good body tension as you hold a balanced start; run and jump to land steady without a stumble or wobble; and organise your direction change.

2 The runs must never be long because the run and jump are of equal importance. Some runs might only need two or three strides if the only space is nearby.

3 A swing up with one arm or leg turns your body towards the other side, often helpful if you are approaching a wall.

### Body

1 The nature of a 'bridge-like shape' can be emphasised by asking the class to point out examples in the hall, to identify the arched shape.

2 Bridges can be held standing with front, back or one side towards the floor; or up-ended on shoulders, head and hands.

3 Variety comes from different supporting parts and different levels. (For example, high on feet; medium on one hand and one foot with one side towards floor; low on heels and shoulders, back towards floor.)

### Arms

1 All weight has to be supported on hands for a second or two. Many will do cartwheels and handstands. Others will do a bunny jump.

2 Each can demonstrate two or three times to ensure at least one good one.

3 'Reflecting and evaluating' is a requirement within National Curriculum Physical Education. Working in pairs enables every pupil to practise this skill without the possible embarrassment of speaking to the whole class.

## Apparatus Work

1 Because this is a simple activity, partners can follow quite close, one behind the other. 'On how many apparatus surfaces can you and your partner perform, with straight arms and bent legs, in the next minute?'

2 Leading partner is responsible for planning to go where both partners will have space to perform the approach, the jump, and the landing and roll.

3 About five minutes are spent practising at each of the three sets of apparatus they will try to visit. This gives time to practise, repeat and improve their sequences. The emphasis is on strong arm support as you travel, alternating with stops at various places to demonstrate a still, bridge-like shape. The still, erect start and finish should be pursued as a way for the performer to signal 'I am ready to start' and 'I have completed my sequence'.

## Final Floor Activity

If a still balance on one foot is beyond anyone's ability, tell them to place the toes of the other foot on the floor to help balance. The balances can be 'different' by holding non-supporting foot in different ways, or by inclining the upper body in different ways, e.g. horizontally forwards, to side, or back.

# Dance

# Introduction to Dance

Dance has a special place in primary school Physical Education because it is intensely physical, sociable, co-operative, creative and expressive. Dance is also great fun and a source of enjoyment for pupils.

The lively, physical nature of Dance is particularly valuable now, when children's lives have become increasingly sedentary and inactive. Well-organised lessons should be vigorous, active and non-stop, because the actions being performed are natural and easy. There are none of the problems encountered when controlling Games implements. There is no potential break in the flow of the lesson as when organising Gymnastic apparatus. In Dance, the teacher should be able to make his or her lessons 'scenes of busy activity.'

It has been said 'If you have never created something, you have never experienced a true sense of contentment.' Creativity is an ever-present feature of Dance and the wise teacher will always recognise, share and praise such achievements.

Teachers with little interest in Physical Education often admit to being impressed by the amount of language heard, used, understood and learned by pupils during Physical Education lessons. This discovery has been a stimulus to those teachers in their subsequent teaching of the subject.

Happily, the 1999 revised version of the National Curriculum still requires schools to include both creative and traditional folk dance. The latter almost completely disappeared during the 1960s and 1970s when education lecturers called folk dance 'quite unsuitable' for primary school pupils because the steps and patterns 'belong to the adult world.'

Whether we are teaching creative or traditional dance, both teacher and class must have a definite 'goal' so that practising can become focused, repeatable, performable – and done expressively, with total commitment and involvement. The challenge to 'find ways to balance', for example, becomes much more exciting and 'real' when the outcome is the tightrope walker in the circus with all the dangerous, unsteady wobbling about in space.

The following lesson plans are designed to provide lots of ideas and practical help to the non-specialist class teacher. It recognises that each revised and reduced version of the NC provides less material, practical help and guidance regarding the content of dance and less help with the nature of good teaching practice in Physical Education. The Teacher Notes that accompany each lesson plan aim to translate Programme of Study, Attainment Target and Learning across the National Curriculum elements into easily understandable objectives as well as giving practical help and guidance with the understanding, organising and teaching of the lessons.

# The aims of Dance

1   Dance is physical and we aim to make lessons physically challenging. The focus is on the body and the development of well-controlled, poised, versatile movement. Vigorous actions also develop strength and flexibility and promote normal, healthy growth and development.

2   Dance is creative and we aim to let pupils use their imagination. Using imagination and skill to plan and present something original makes Dance a most satisfying activity. When a pupil's capacity for creative thinking and action is recognised and appreciated by the teacher, and shared with the class, this can increase self-confidence and self-esteem.

3   Dance is expressive and communicative, and we aim to let pupils express their inner feelings through outward movement. We use our bodies to 'express and communicate ideas' (NC Programme of Study). Feelings are expressed through body movement, as in angry stamping of feet; joyful gesturing of arms – 'Goal!'; fear, with its tight withdrawal of the whole body; or the swaggering shoulders and strides of the over-confident.

4   Dance is artistic and we aim to include variety and contrasts in every lesson. Knowledge and understanding of the elements that enhance the quality of a performance need to be taught, and they contribute to a pupil's artistic education. Variety and contrast in the use of body action, shape, speed, force, level and direction are major contributors to improved quality.

5   Dance is sociable, friendly and co-operative and we aim to let pupils work alone, with a partner and in groups in a variety of roles. Because movement is natural, without the difficulty of controlling unpredictable Games implements, success is quickly achieved. This achievement is often shared with a partner or group, leading to a strong sense of 'togetherness'; unselfish sharing of space; taking turns; demonstrating to and being demonstrated to; and being appreciated by others' comments are all typical of Dance teaching.

6   Dance is fun and we aim to make enjoyment a constant feature. Enjoyment from being praised for achievement; from participating and interacting in such an interesting and sociable activity; and from feeling and looking better after exercise, can all have a significant influence on peoples' eventual choice of lifestyle in years to come.

# The creative Dance lesson Plan

**Warming-up activities** aim to inspire an enjoyable, lively start to the lesson and put the class in the mood for Dance. The activities need to be simple enough to get the class working, almost immediately, often by following the teacher who calls out and demonstrates the activities, which do not need to relate to the main theme or emphasis of the lesson.

Some form of travelling, using the feet, is the usual warming-up activity, with a specific way of moving being asked for. It might be to demonstrate better use of space, greater variety, greater control, good poise and body tension, or simply an enthusiastic use of all body parts to warm up.

The teacher, here, is a stimulating 'purveyor of action' enthusiastically leading the whole class, often by example, into whole-hearted participation in simple activities, needing little explanation.

**Teaching and developing movement skills and patterns** to be used in the new dance follows the warm-up. Teaching methods include challenging, questioning, use of good demonstrations, and direct teaching:

**a** 'Kneel down and curl to your smallest shape. Show me how you can start to grow, very slowly. Are you starting with your back, head, shoulders, elbows or arms? Show me clearly how you rise to a full, wide stretched position.'

**b** 'How are the bubbles (made by teacher and pupils) moving? Where are they going? Floating gently, gliding smoothly, soaring from low to higher, sinking slowly?'

Here, the teacher is an educator, informing, challenging, questioning, using demonstrations and sometimes using direct teaching.

**Creating and performing the dance** finishes off the lesson:

**a** 'Slowly, start to grow and show me which parts are leading as you rise to your full, wide flower shape in our "Spring" dance. You might even twist your flower shape to look at the sun.'

**b** 'For our "Bubbles" dance, I will say the four actions that we have practised – floating, gliding, soaring, sinking – slowly, and you will show me how you have planned to dance them.'

The teacher, now, is a coach, helping and guiding the pupils as they work at their creation, moving around to all parts of the room to advise, encourage, enthuse, praise, and, eventually, present and lead the thanks to them for their demonstrations.

Depending on its complexity, a dance will be repeated two to four times to allow sufficient time for repetition, practice and improvement to take place, and a satisfactory performance to be achieved and presented.

# Developing Dance Movement

To avoid confusion, the teacher will be thinking about, looking for, and talking about one element of movement at a time. In the early stages of a lesson's development, the teacher should only look at the actions and how the body parts concerned perform them. This allows an opportunity for progress and improvement. If, however, the teacher is exhorting the class to think about 'your spacing, actions, shape, speed – and what about some direction changes?', all at the same time, then confusion will be the only outcome.

### Stage 1  The Body
What is the child doing?

**1**  Actions – travelling, jumping, turning, rolling, balancing, gesturing, rising, falling, etc.

**2**  Body parts – legs, feet, hands, shoulders, head, etc.

**3**  Body shape – stretched, curled, wide, twisted, arched.

### Stage 2  The Space
Where is the child doing it?

**1**  Directions – forwards, backwards, sideways.

**2**  Level – high, medium, low.

**3**  Size – own, little, personal space; whole room, large, general space, shared with others.

### Stage 3  The Quality
How is the child doing it?

1   Weight or effort – firm, strong, vigorous, heavy.

2   Time or speed – sudden, fast, explosive, speeding up; slow, still, slowing down.

### Stage 4  The Relationships
With whom is the child doing it?

1   Alone – but always conscious of sharing space with others.

2   Teacher – near, following, mirroring, in a circle with, away from, back towards.

3   Partner – leading, following, meeting, parting, mirroring, copying, touching.

4   Group – circle, part of class for a demonstration.

# Teaching Methods

Enthusiastic teaching is the main inspiration behind a successful lesson and usually creates an equally enthusiastic response in pupils.

The lesson plan is the busy teacher's essential guide. Failure to work from a written-down plan can result in repetition of lessons. July's lesson will only be more advanced than the previous September's if all the lessons in between have been recorded and referred to.

'Shared choice' or 'indirect' teaching is the lesson plan most often used. The teacher decides the nature of the activity and challenges the class to decide on the actions. 'As you travel and stop to my tambourine beat, can you show me varied travelling actions, and clear, still, body shapes?'

Shared choice teaching with its 'Can you show me...?' approach produces a wide variety of results to add to the repertoire of both class and teacher. The NC requirement that pupils should be able to demonstrate that they can plan and 'use skills, actions and ideas appropriately' is best achieved through shared choice.

'Direct' teaching takes place when the teacher tells the class what to do. For example: 'Skip to visit every part of the room...'; 'Stand with feet apart. Slowly stretch your arms high above your head.' If the class are restless, unresponsive or doing poor work, a directed activity can restore interest and discipline, and provide ideas and starting points from which to develop. Less creative pupils will benefit from direct teaching.

Pupil demonstrations are essential teaching aids because we remember what we see – good quality, safe, correct ways to perform, and good examples of variety and interesting contrasts. Occasional pupil demonstrations with follow-up comments by the observing pupils often bring out points not noticed by the teacher. Making friendly, encouraging, helpful comments to classmates is good for class morale and for extending the class repertoire.

'Be found working, not waiting' is a motto the class should have been trained to understand and pursue in order to enjoy satisfactory lessons with sufficient time for the creative dance, which is the climax of the lesson.

Praise and recognition of progress and good work are important teaching aids, particularly when given with enthusiasm. Words of praise should be specific because they are heard by all and remind the class of the main points: 'Well done, Emma. Your floating snowflake movement was light and gentle.'

It has been said that 'Dance is all about making, remembering and repeating patterns'. Whether we are performing a created dance or an existing folk dance, there will be a still start and finish and an arrangement of repeated parts within.

# Examples of Dance Lesson Development

If the class teacher feels confident about progressing the dance beyond the Stage 1 question 'What actions is the child doing?', the supplementary questions are those we should ask when observing movement.

### Stage 1 – What are the body parts doing? What shapes are being used?

○  *Autumn Leaves* – the whole body makes the leaf shape, which may have parts curling in, parts sticking out, be both smooth and crinkly

○  *Puppet Makers* – the puppet's arms can bend, swing, circle or reach up into a long or wide stretched shape

○  *Fireworks* – the arms can reach forwards to give the whole body a streamlined rocket shape.

**Stage 2 – Where are we doing the dance?  The floor is our stage – how are we using it to make our dance more interesting and exciting?**

○ *Autumn Leaves* – as they fly they will sometimes soar from low to high; rotate in the same space; hover, hardly moving; glide to a far corner; drop straight, or with a spiralling action

○ *Puppet Makers* – will show their puppets how hands and feet can reach into the space in front, at the side, behind and overhead

○ *Fireworks* – the rocket's straight swoosh contrasting with the spinning, circling of the Catherine wheel, and the unpredictable jumping and shifting of the bangers.

**Stage 3 – How are the movements being performed? Are the right amounts of force, effort, speed and quality factors being applied to make the performance particularly attractive, surprising, expressive?**

○ *Autumn Leaves* – the slow, gentle rise and fall, still attached to the branch, contrasts with the sudden, almost explosive snap and break away from the branch

○ *Puppet Makers* – arms can circle and swing, gently and softly, or they can punch and gesture in the air space, firmly and strongly

○ *Fireworks* – the long, smooth, ongoing, neat zoom of the rising rocket contrasts with the sudden, explosive, fragmented scattering.

**Stage 4 – With whom are we dancing? What are our relationships with the others in the room?**

○ *Autumn Leaves* – an individual dance but we share the space with others as we weave, swoop, soar, hover, glide, tilt and turn, in and out, alongside or around them

○ *Puppet Makers* – puppet and maker mirror each other on the spot, lead and follow, or are attached with strings in the travelling

○ *Fireworks* – one group at a time performs until spent, together, in the bonfire. All combine to flicker and sparkle in the fire, and interweave, flickering, shooting, crackling, subsiding, dying.

# National Curriculum requirements for Dance – Key Stage 1: the main features

'The government believes that two hours of physical activity a week, including the National Curriculum for Physical Education and extra-curricular activities, should be an aspiration for all schools. This applies to all key stages.'

## Programme of Study

Pupils should be taught to:

a   use movement imaginatively, responding to stimuli, including music, and performing basic skills (e.g. travelling, being still, making a shape, jumping, turning, gesturing)
b   change the rhythm, speed, level and direction of their movements
c   create and perform dances using simple movement patterns, including those from different times and cultures
d   express and communicate ideas and feelings.

## Attainment Targets

Pupils should be able to demonstrate that they can:

a   select and use skills, actions and ideas appropriately, applying them with co-ordination and control
b   copy, explore, repeat and remember skills, and link them in ways that suit the activities
c   talk about differences between their own and others' work; suggest improvements; and use this understanding to improve their performance.

## Main NC Headings when considering assessment, progression and expectation

**Planning** – mostly before performing, but planning also takes place during performance, with pupils making quick decisions to find a space or adapt a skill. In these initial, exploratory stages, pupils try things out and learn from early efforts. When planning is satisfactory, there is evidence of understanding of the task; good use of own ideas; and consideration for others sharing the space.

**Performing and improving performance** – always the main outcome to be achieved. When performing is satisfactory, there is evidence of well-controlled, neat, safe and thoughtful work; a capacity for almost non-stop work, alone and with others; and simple skills being performed accurately and linked together with increasing control.

**Linking actions** – pupils build longer, 'joined-up' sequences of linked actions in response to the task set and stimuli used. In the same way that joined-up words make language and joined-up notes make music, joined-up actions produce movement sequences, ideally with a clear and obvious beginning, middle and end.

**Reflecting and making judgements** – pupils describe what they and others have done; talk about what they liked in a performance; and then make practical use of this reflection to improve. Where standards in evaluating are satisfactory, there is evidence of accurate observation and awareness of the actions; understanding of differences and similarities seen in demonstrations; awareness of key features and ways to achieve and improve them; and sensitive concern for others' feelings when discussing them.

## Assessment

There are three main requirements within the Attainment Target to concentrate on when assessing achievement. The dual emphasis on both performing and learning involves pupils in the continuous, inter-related process of: planning; performing; reflecting/evaluating.

   **Planning** provides the focus and the concentrated thinking necessary for an accurate performance. It takes place both before and during performances, and subsequent performances are influenced by the planning that takes place after individuals and the group reflect on the success or otherwise of the activity.

   Where planning standards are satisfactory, there is evidence of:

a   thinking ahead and visualising the intended outcome
b   originality and variety – individual ideas
c   unselfish, considerate sharing of space

**d** positive personal qualities such as enthusiasm, concentration, and whole-hearted involvement

**e** a clear understanding of the task

**f** good judgements being made.

**Performing** is the most important feature. We are fortunate that the visual nature of Physical Education enables pupils' achievements to be easily seen and judged. When standards in performing are satisfactory, there is evidence of:

**a** neat, accurate, 'correct' performances

**b** successful, safe outcomes

**c** originality and versatility

**d** consistency and the ability to repeat and remember

**e** adaptability, making sudden adjustments as required

**f** economy of effort, making everything look 'easy'.

**Reflecting and evaluating** are important because they help both the performers and the observers with their further planning, preparation, adaptation and improvement. When standards in evaluating are satisfactory, pupils are able to:

**a** observe accurately and pick out key features

**b** make encouraging, helpful comments about a performance

**c** make comparisons between two or more performers

**d** comment on the 'correctness' of a performance

**e** suggest ways in which the work might be improved.

# Year 2 Dance programme

Pupils should be able to:

| Autumn | Spring | Summer |
|---|---|---|
| **1** Dress safely and sensibly.<br><br>**2** Respond readily and quickly to instructions. Keep practising.<br><br>**3** Improve basic actions by adding clear shapes and good poise.<br><br>**4** Work hard to make the lessons 'scenes of busy activity'.<br><br>**5** Become body-parts aware – feet, ankles, legs, hands, arms, shoulders – and link actions in short, repeating patterns.<br><br>**6** Experience working with a range of stimuli – actions, body parts, fireworks, music, poems, partner, Christmas.<br><br>**7** Demonstrate ability to plan and perform a series of joined-up actions, neatly.<br><br>**8** Link these movements with increasing control by using changes of direction, level, speed and tension.<br><br>**9** Demonstrate knowledge and understanding through actions.<br><br>**10** Celebrate 'Fireworks' with good use of shape, speed, effort and direction as in rockets, Catherine wheels and bangers.<br><br>**11** Celebrate Christmas with 'Puppet Makers', making a simple story, expressing the weary maker, the happy puppets and the excitement of the chase.<br><br>**12** Describe what they and others have done and how they did it. | **1** Perform simple, basic actions such as travelling, jumping, turning and stillness, with positive, confident, correct, poised use of the body.<br><br>**2** Experience and be guided in making dances with clear beginnings, middles and ends.<br><br>**3** Demonstrate increasing confidence over use of shape, space and effort.<br><br>**4** Plan a 'Winter' dance with a partner and percussion, based on three seasonal winter words on a card.<br><br>**5** Demonstrate how good use of contrasts enhances a dance, as in winter's 'Freeze' and 'Melt'.<br><br>**6** Co-operate with a partner, often observing, commenting and, sometimes, suggesting how to improve a performance.<br><br>**7** Learn traditional dance steps and figures, and simple international circle dances, where class can see teacher.<br><br>**8** Create simple characters and little stories in response to music. Explore feelings.<br><br>**9** Describe simple actions seen, using simple terms to describe. | **1** Demonstrate good body control in travelling, jumping and stillness.<br><br>**2** Demonstrate an enthusiasm and ability to practise to improve.<br><br>**3** Respond rhythmically to music with skill, poise, balance and co-ordination.<br><br>**4** Be given opportunities to explore moods and feelings through structured tasks.<br><br>**5** Create simple characters, expressing them through their body movements.<br><br>**6** Work often with a partner to improve and extend the skills learned and to share in creating something bigger than can be achieved alone.<br><br>**7** Link movements to demonstrate an understanding of the elements of 'movement' – shape, space, effort, speed.<br><br>**8** Make a seasonal 'Nature' dance to show how animals or plants come into being. Kittens or lambs are examples of well-known stimuli, inspiring lively action.<br><br>**9** Demonstrate knowledge and understanding mainly through physical actions rather than verbal expression.<br><br>**10** Learn and perform a simple, traditional British circle dance, and revise other folk dances learned previously.<br><br>**11** Work harder for longer with greater confidence, control and versatility.<br><br>**12** Express moods and feelings in a three-part dance about infant school days – shy start; good middle; brilliant end.<br><br>**13** Make simple, friendly judgements on how others have performed. |

# Lesson Plan 1 • 25 minutes
### September

**Theme:** *Awareness of basic actions and contrasts of shape.*

## Warm-up Activities
### 5 minutes

Let's all join hands in a nice, big, round circle to sing and move together:

*Let's join hands in one big ring,* (arms swing forwards and back)
*Let's join hands and let us sing,* (add knees bend and stretch)
*Let's join hands both high and low,* (arms swing high at same time as knees stretch)
*Let's drop hands and wave 'Hello!'*

*Let's all bounce in one big ring,* (quiet, springy, upward jumps)
*Let's all bounce and bounce and sing,*
*Let's keep bouncing, nice and slow,*
*Now shake hands and say 'Hello!'*

## Movement Skills Training
### 15 minutes

1   Well done, singers and dancers. That was a lively, friendly way to start. Stand in your own good space, now, and show me some of the actions that we can do on the spot to this lively, jazzy music.

2   I can see walking; marching; bouncing; skipping; stamping; running; balancing by rising and lowering on tiptoes. Practise, thinking of actions that use your feet and legs.

3   Be very clever now and add a body movement to whatever you are doing with your feet and legs. For example – stepping and clapping; bouncing and turning; stamping and gesturing. Remember, we are working on the spot – not travelling!

4   Let's look at some very good examples now.

5   Using the same lively music, let me see you travelling to visit all parts of the room. All together... best walking... best skipping... best bouncing... best hopping...

6   As you travel this time, show me different body shapes to make it more interesting. Ready... Go!... walking (tall, arms stretched upwards or feet and arms wide)... skipping (curled with arms in to sides or high, stretched leading arm and leg)... bouncing (twisted with upper body facing behind or very straight body and arms at sides)... hopping (curled, wide or stretched).

## Dance — The Snake
### 10 minutes

1   Find a partner and stand, one behind the other, to make a little snake whose front actions will be copied by its back part. A snake's actions ripple down its body from head to tail.

2   Leaders, you are going to take your partner to different parts of the room, always looking for good spaces. Show your partner two or three actions and clear shapes to copy. Keep repeating those different actions so that you can remember them. Go!

3   Well done. Your snakes kept travelling beautifully and you are repeating your little pattern of two or three actions. Change places. The new leader can add an action on the spot before leading in to your two or three travelling actions. Begin.

4   Practice; performance; comments; improved practice.

**Dance**

# Teaching notes and NC guidance
# Development over 3 lessons

Pupils should be taught to:

**a** respond readily to instructions

**b** be physically active

**c** be mindful of others

**d** be aware of the safety risks of inappropiate clothing, footwear and jewellery.

At the start of the school year, the lesson's main emphases include:

**a** establishing a tradition of immediate and whole-hearted responses to instructions. Good behaviour, expressed in listening quietly and then doing what was asked, is essential if all, including the teacher, are to enjoy action-filled, almost non-stop lessons;

**b** aiming to make lessons 'scenes of busy activity', with everyone working and no-one waiting. The instant-action starting song in the circle where all can see the teacher; the lively travelling with teacher direction in the middle part of the lesson; and the simple, ongoing, partners travelling dance climax, all contribute to near non-stop action;

**c** working together sensibly and co-operatively, unselfishly sharing the floor space, and expressing pleasure and appreciation for demonstrations by others;

**d** all being safely and sensibly dressed.

## Warm-up Activities

The teacher demonstrates two of the lines at a time, with the class watching and listening. Teacher and class repeat the sets of two lines, singing and moving, together.

## Movement Skills Training

**1–4** From thinking of, and practising actions on the spot, using feet and legs, pupils are challenged to add in a body movement as they were doing in the warm-up. A demonstration is essential to share the many body-and-legs dual actions that will be presented by an enthusiastic class.

**5–6** From showing best travelling actions as they visit all parts of the room, pupils are now challenged to travel in a variety of ways, and include varied and interesting body shapes. The 'training', here, is in the development of an awareness of the basic travelling actions and the many contrasting body shapes that can accompany them.

## The Snake Dance

**1** The pairs are asked to stand about one metre apart so the follower can see the leader's feet, legs, body actions and shapes easily.

**2** The teacher also emphasises that each of the two or three actions being repeated as a sequence should only last a few seconds, or for three or four travelling steps. (Unless restrained, many 'travellers' will go all around the hall, using one action only.)

**3** The new leader can add a favourite action on the spot before repeating the sequence of two or three actions already created and practised.

**4** Performing for others and receiving comments from others is the ideal climax to a lesson.

# Lesson Plan 2 • 30 minutes
## September/October

**Theme:** *Body parts awareness.*

## Warm-up Activities
### 5 minutes

1  I will read this poem slowly. Listen carefully and show me how well you can do the actions:

*Nod your head, bend your knees,*
*Grow as tall as Christmas trees.*
*On your knees, slowly fall,*
*Curl yourself into a ball.*
*Raise your head, jump up like so,*
*Wave your hand and say 'Hello!'*

2  I will read the poem once again. Help me with the words if you remember them. Think about all the different ways our clever bodies can move.

## Movement Skills Training
### 15 minutes

1  You danced to the poem beautifully – and remembered lots of the words. Let's see if we can practise, then remember, sets of three actions. Use your feet first. They are very important parts in movement.

2  Bounce your heels a little way off the floor, toes touching the floor. Bounce heels, bounce heels, 3, 4; bounce low, bounce low, 3, 4; springy, springy, springy, stop! Now step smartly with a lift of your front leg. Step, step, 3 and 4; stepping smartly, 3 and 4.

3  Stay where you are and stamp firmly. Stamp, stamp, 3 and 4; on the spot, 3, 4; bump, bump, bump for 4; stamp, stamp, 3 and stop!

4  Perform all three parts again, four counts to each. Ready? Bounce, bounce, heels bounce; step forwards, 3, 4; stamp, stamp, start again. Bounce, 2, 3, 4; step, 2, 3, 4; stamp, 2, 3 and stop! Good. We all kept together.

5  Hands and arms now, clapping first. Clap, 2, 3, again. Clap, 2, 3, 4. Clap, 2, 3, 4. Now let arms swing forwards and back, just like when we walk. Swings, swings, lively swings; 1, 2, 3, 4. Again, and let your shoulders twist to make the swings bigger. Swing, swing, big swings; reach, reach, 3 and 4.

6  Shake hands – as if you were shaking them to dry them. Shake, shake, shake, shake; 1, 2, 3, 4; dry them, 2, 3, 4; quick-shake, 2, 3, stop!

## Dance — Clever Feet and Hands
### 10 minutes

1  Listen to the rhythm of the music. 1, 2, 3, 4; 1, 2, 3, 4. Keep that speed as you bounce, step, stamp for four counts. Think about and 'feel' your feet. Go! Bounce, bounce, 3, 4; step 2, 3, 4; stamp on the spot, 3, 4; bounce, 2, 3, 4; step, 2, 3, 4; stamp, 2, 3 and stop!

2  That was excellent. Three very different leg actions. Now hands only. Clap, 2, 3, 4; swing, 2, 3, 4; shake, 2, 3, 4; clap, 2, 3, 4; swing, 2, 3, 4; shake, 2, 3 and stop! Good, everyone.

3  Now, can you be very clever and join together the three leg and the three hand actions? With the music, begin. Bounce-clap, bounce-clap, bounce-clap, 4; step-swing, step-swing, step-swing, 4; stamp-shake, stamp-shake, stamp-shake, 4. (Repeat for practice.)

4  Well done. This is very difficult and you managed it splendidly. We could call our dance 'Clever Hands and Feet and Clever Girls and Boys!' Let's have half the class looking at and enjoying the other half. Then we can talk about the things we particularly liked.

**Dance**

# Teaching notes and NC guidance
## Development over 3 lessons

Pupils should be able to show control in linking actions together in ways that suit the activities.

Being able to plan and perform a series of joined-up actions neatly and with control is the main requirement within the National Curriculum. If a pupil can remember and repeat such a sequence, he or she is proving the ability to:

**a**  plan, showing an understanding of what was asked for

**b**  perform more than one skill at a time by linking actions thoughtfully

**c**  be able to practise and improve his or her performance.

The pattern of performing joined-up actions runs right through the lesson, as it should do right through infant school. There are eight simple actions in the warm-up, all stimulated and given a rhythm by the spoken poem.

Three sets of joined-up actions on the spot – bouncing, stepping and stamping – have a repeated rhythm, medium-speed music accompaniment in the middle of the lesson, expanded in the dance climax by adding hand and arm claps, swings and shakes. Success at this requires the total attention and whole-hearted effort sought in the previous lesson.

## Warm-up Activities

1  The class can listen to two lines at a time read by the teacher. When the two lines are repeated by the teacher, the class can perform the actions.

2  Saying the words, and thinking about the many and varied actions involved and being practised, aim to develop body-parts awareness through feeling and doing.

## Movement Skills Training

**1–4**  Pupils are praised for remembering the words in the warm-up and challenged to perform and remember the three actions – bouncing, stepping and stamping – practised in sets of three counts within a repeating pattern.

**5–6**  From awareness of what feet were doing, the awareness, now, is of actions the hands can perform – clapping, swinging and shaking – still within a three-part repeating pattern.

## Clever Feet and Hands Dance

1  Music is introduced to give a repeating, four-count, rhythmic accompaniment to the three feet-and-leg actions sequences. Pupils are asked to 'feel' the bouncing, stepping and stamping.

2  The three-part, hands-only sequence of clapping, swinging and shaking is revised.

3  'Clever Feet and Hands' are now challenged to perform a sequence of three joined-up pairs of joined-up hands and feet actions, all in time with the rhythmic music.

4  Being able to remember, repeat, improve and present the three sets of pairs of actions is most commendable. Pupils look forward to and work hard for the demonstrations that they present, observe, comment on and learn from.

# Lesson Plan 3 • 30 minutes
## November

**Theme:** *Fireworks.*

## Warm-up Activities
### 5 minutes

In our last lesson we created a 'Clever Feet and Hands' dance. Let's start by doing some movements that use most parts of our body. Swing the arms forwards and back, then forwards and high above your head. Bend the knees and swing the arms down to let your hands brush the floor as they swing back. Arms then swing forwards and up above the head with knees and body stretching. Again. Swing forwards, back, and forwards and up; bend down, swing arms back and forwards, and high up again. Keep practising your swinging, bending and stretching.

## Movement Skills Training
### 15 minutes

1 What words describe a rocket's action? Whoosh? Zoom? Bang?

2 What do these actions look like? Fast, straight, streamlined?

3 Before the rocket takes off we need to light the paper fuse. It splutters and sizzles, then the long thin rocket shoots off, soaring from low to high.

4 Everyone, ready for your low, thin, streamlined start in your rocket shape. Where will you zoom to? Ready? Go!

5 How will you explode? From small to big with a scatter of your whole body? Get ready to explode, scatter and fall down. Go!

6 Let's practise again as you splutter and sizzle . . . Zoom, Whoosh . . . explode and scatter . . . twinkle, fall, glide down.

7 What are the movements of a Catherine wheel? A slow spin at the start gradually speeds up and throws out sparks. Then it slows down gradually and dies. Try the Catherine wheel movements and use your arms for spinning to stop you becoming dizzy. Show me your slow start, your speeding up, your slowing and dying.

8 What actions do the little bangers make you think of? Shooting and jumping here and there, unexpectedly in an uneven way.

9 Let me see your pattern of unexpected, quick jumping and running actions. Surprise me. Go!

10 Let's try each of the fireworks again and show me the main thing about each one. Ready, rockets? Go! Catherine wheels, go! Bangers, go! Well done. One more practice and you can accompany yourselves with your own sounds. Go!

## Dance — Fireworks
### 10 minutes

1 That was excellent. You pleased me and surprised me. Now, you choose which one you want to be. Hands up . . . rockets . . . Catherine wheels . . . bangers. Catherine wheels go first. Go! . . . Now die away.

2 As the last Catherine wheel starts to slow... jumping bangers start now.

3 When the last two bangers only are left... Rockets sizzle, zoom, bang and scatter down like stars. Alternative ending – one rocket can stray and land in the middle of the room among all the spent fireworks lying there. The whole group can represent the unlit bonfire and start to flicker like sparks and flames, with twitching elbows and shoulders, making little fires all over. Own vocal accompaniment can be used. 'Crackle... shoot... flicker...' Slowly, the bonfire becomes quieter and dies.

**Dance**

# Teaching notes and NC guidance
# Development over 4 lessons

Pupils should be taught to develop control, co-ordination, balance, poise and elevation in the basic actions of travelling, jumping, turning, gesturing and stillness.

From the 'Clever Feet and Hands' dance of the previous lesson, we move on to clever whole bodies, working expressively to represent varied fireworks actions.

Everyone practises the three different actions in the middle of the lesson, with much questioning by the teacher to inspire a thoughtful, planned, focused response. A repeating pattern of each action is asked for so that the performers are able to remember, repeat, improve and express the movement characteristics of each one.

The dance climax, to which all the practising has led, does call for stillness while waiting one's turn; then exciting, whole-body travelling and zooming, spinning and turning, shooting and jumping; and finally gestures, as pupils shoot, explode, whirl, leap about, then crackle and flicker.

## Warm-up Activities

The whole body swinging, bending and stretching can be referred to as 'our ski-swing action warm-up' and uses most joint and muscle groups, taking them to their full extension. A vocal accompaniment of 'Swish! Swish!' can be used with the long arm swings.

## Movement Skills Training

In contrast to the direct teaching of the previous lesson where the pupils were given the exact nature of the bounces, steps and stamps by the teacher (e.g. 'bounce low, springy'; 'step smartly with lift of front foot', etc.), the teacher is now continually challenging and questioning the class to make them think about and plan their own responses, asking: 'What kind of actions?' (rockets, Catherine wheel, little bangers),'Where will you zoom to?' and challenging 'Show me...'; 'Let me see...'. In this shared-choice teaching style the teacher decides the nature of the activity and the class decide the actual actions. Shared choice leads to a wide variety of results and an expanded class and teacher repertoire. The wide use of imagery and imagination helps the class to express themselves more clearly. 'Zooming' when imagining that you are moving like a rocket makes the action much easier to express than if you are simply trying to zoom as a way of travelling.

## Fireworks Dance

The dance performance climax of the lesson is a good example of a shared-choice presentation. Pupils decide which firework they will represent and the teacher decides the order of the dance itself – Catherine wheel start; jumping bangers middle; and rockets ending. The teacher is the main observer of the whole dance, but each of the three groups can watch the other two while waiting their turn to start, or after performing.

# Year 2

# Lesson Plan 4 • 30 minutes
## December

**Theme:** *Christmas and toys.*

## Warm-up Activities
### 5 minutes

1 Find a partner for 'Follow My Leader'. The leader pretends the partner is just learning to move and has to be shown, very carefully, how to use the different parts of the body. Make your movements 'larger than life' and let's see if you can make a little pattern of three actions, exactly together.

2 Following partner, you lead now and show me your 'larger than life' ways to move feet, legs, arms, shoulders, or the whole body.

## Movement Skills Training
### 15 minutes

1 Keep the same partner, well spaced out all over the room, facing each other. One of you will be the puppet maker with your hammer and chisel. The other will be the still, solid block of wood.

2 Puppet maker, chisel out the head shape. Show your puppet how a head can move up, down, side to side, and rotate. Puppet, copy.

3 Puppet maker, work on the shoulders and show how they can lift and lower, go forwards and back, and do circular motions.

4 Arms are shaped next with long, up-and-down chisel movements. The bending, stretching, swinging and circling are then copied.

5 The body shape and the big body movements of bending, stretching, twisting and turning are made and demonstrated.

6 Legs are the most important body part. The puppet maker has to crouch low to shape out the legs and feet. Big actions of bending to the front and sides and swinging are shown and copied on the spot.

7 Legs can do much more than swing, bend and step on the spot. They can take you to all parts of the room. Some puppet makers choose to do 'Follow My Leader' with their puppets. Others, with hands high above the puppet's head, suspend them from strings. Mirroring or dangling, the puppets are guided through the varied travelling actions. They walk, skip, run, hop, bounce, jump with full use of the neck, arms, shoulders and legs just created.

## Dance — Puppet Makers
### 10 minutes

Music: Beethoven's 9th, Choral Symphony – *Ode to Joy* (2 mins 18 secs)

1 From the beginning with the still, solid lump of wood, the puppet makers hammer and chisel the shape of head, shoulders, arms, body, feet and legs. At each stage, they demonstrate and lead the growing puppet through the body movements of each. Puppet makers travel with their own puppets as they visit all parts of the room. Movements are 'larger than life'.

2 All this hammering, chiselling and moving has been hard work. The puppets are hung up on a hook in the workshop and the puppet makers lie down for a well-earned rest and sleep on the floor.

3 The puppets have enjoyed their play-like travels so much that they jump down off their wall hooks and all dance round.

4 The puppet makers waken and are angry to see their puppets out of place. They chase after their own puppet who dodges away.

5 Puppets are caught and gripped firmly with one hand. The other hand points and gestures 'Naughty puppet! Behave yourself!'

**Dance**

# Teaching notes and NC guidance
## Development over 4 lessons

Pupils should be taught to explore feelings and develop their response to music through Dance by using rhythmic responses. Pupils should be able to improve performance, through practice, alone and with a partner.

In this easy dance the pupils can almost be talked through the whole dance by the teacher, who guides them through the timings of each part. 'Chisel out the head shape, front, sides, back, top. Now show your puppet how its head can move. Puppets, watch and copy.' A repeating pattern at each stage will be helpful in remembering, repeating and improving the dance. 'Show your puppet how legs can swing forwards and back, forwards and back; step, step on the spot; swing to one side, swing to other side; swing forwards and back, forwards and back; step, step, on the spot; swing to one side, swing to other side.'

'Feelings' being expressed will include the weariness of the hard-working puppet makers as they sag slowly to rest on the floor; the happiness of the puppets as they travel and try out all the enjoyable play-like movements possible in their clever bodies; the surprise and annoyance of the puppet makers when they waken and see the badly behaved puppets at the games of chase.

## Warm-up Activities

Partners face each other, a metre apart, and perform large movements of body parts slowly, allowing partners to keep exactly together. A varied, repeating, linked trio of activities might include one for legs; one for arms; and one for the whole body.

## Movement Skills Training

The teacher, with a partner, but without any music, demonstrates briefly the pattern of chiselling each part, and then showing the growing puppet how that part can move. 'No touching any part of your partner as you make head, shoulders, arms, body or legs' must be emphasised or pupils will make contact with their imaginary hammers and chisels.

## Puppet Makers Dance

1   With the music now, and with the teacher's continuous reminder of the body parts to be demonstrated by the puppet maker and practised by the emerging puppet, the complete puppet is built out of the starting block of wood. 'Hold your puppet on a string, walking behind the puppet' is the reminder as the finished puppet is allowed to travel, using all the body parts to try them out while moving. We want these movements to be 'larger than life' once again.

2–3 Hard-working, tired puppet makers hang their puppets on a hook and lie down for their well-earned rest. Like young children, the puppets jump from their hooks and dance all around the room.

4–5 Puppet makers, disturbed by the sound of puppets dashing around, jump up and chase after their own puppet. When the music stops, the puppet makers catch and hold their puppet.

# Lesson Plan 5 • 30 minutes
## January

**Theme:** *Winter.*

## Warm-up Activities
### 5 minutes

Let's sing and move to keep warm, pretending we are outside:

*This is the way we skip to keep warm,*
*skip to keep warm, skip to keep warm,*
*This is the way we skip to keep warm,*
*on a cold and frosty morning*

*This is the way we big bend and stretch,*
*big bend and stretch, big bend and stretch,*
    *(bend knees to touch floor, high stretch)*
*This is the way we big bend and stretch,*
*on a cold and frosty morning.*

(Repeat several times.)

## Movement Skills Training
### 15 minutes

1   If I asked you to do a 'Winter' drawing, what would you do?

2   'Snowflakes falling' is a good answer, thank you. Can you all move like a snowflake, slowly, gently, turning, hovering, falling?

3   'Wind bending the trees' is another good answer, thank you. Show me how the wind's strong, big, rushing movement is different from the snowflake's.

4   'Ice in a stream' is another excellent answer, thank you. Let me see you flowing like a stream. When I call 'Freeze!' show me how quickly you can stiffen into your rigid, jagged, icy shape.

## Dance — Winter
### 10 minutes

| | | | |
|---|---|---|---|
| WIND | SWOOSH | WHIRL | DROP |
| SNOWFLAKE | FLOAT | HOVER | SINK |
| STREAM | RUSH | FREEZE | MELT |

1   Find a partner. One of you will collect a card and the other will pick up a piece of percussion.

2   Find a good floor space and look at the three action words on your card. Please do not look at other couples' cards. Three different cards are being used for our 'Winter' dance. Each card also tells you what is doing the three actions.

3   Dancing partner, perform your three actions carefully for your partner to watch and then make helpful comments. Start when ready – without any percussion sounds at this stage.

4   Well done. Dancers, sit down and be given some friendly, helpful advice to improve your performance. Were the actions clear? Were the body shapes full and clear? Was the speed right?

5   The same dancer again, please. Partner with percussion, you may quietly accompany your partner, starting and stopping to make the three actions separate. Begin when ready, please.

6   Well done, everyone. The improvements were obvious. Now change places. No accompaniment this time. New dancer, begin when ready.

7   Dancers, sit down and listen to the helpful comments.

8   Same dancers practise again, using the good advice received.

**Dance**

# Teaching notes and NC guidance
# Development over 4 lessons

Pupils should be involved in the continuous process of planning, performing and evaluating.

As well as asking him or herself, 'Was my lesson filled with worthwhile, enjoyable and challenging activity, flowing almost non-stop from start to finish?' the teacher also needs to check, 'Did I provide opportunities for thoughtful planning, challenging the pupils to think ahead to try to see an intended outcome? Did the lesson build up to an end-of-lesson performance of a created dance? Somewhere in the lesson did I provide opportunities for the class to see a demonstration and make friendly, helpful comments, evaluating what they had seen?'

In the shared-choice teaching method used in the lesson, the teacher, with the help of action words on cards, decides the nature of the activity. The pupils then plan and decide the precise actions to be practised, repeated, improved and eventually presented. The observing partner has to watch carefully to identify the main feature of the actions, reflect on their accuracy, and then sensitively suggest ways to bring about an improvement.

## Warm-up Activities

With an instant start, the teacher sings out the words of this well-known poem and starts to perform the actions which the class will immediately start to copy. Other ideas for keeping warm in winter might include 'This is the way we dance in the hall, dance in the hall' and 'This is the way we chase outside, chase outside.'

## Movement Skills Training

From moving bodies trying to keep warm in winter, we move on to imagery and trying to express wintry features suggested by the class, imagining how they might move. Such use of imagination makes the actions 'like snowflakes, trees in the wind, ice in a stream' much easier to understand, plan and represent. The teacher's 'Show me...; Can you...?; Let me see...' challenges the class to produce focused, thoughtful, varied, good-quality movements.

## Winter Dance

**1–3** One partner sits with the card on the floor in front of him or her. The dancing partner stands beside the inactive one, ready to dance onto the small 'stage' in front of them. The dancing partner performs each of the three actions for a time limit set by the teacher. 'First action to bring you on to your little stage... go! Second action... begin! Final action... now!'

**4–5** Dancers sit down beside the observing partners to be given encouragement for good points, and help to make the dance better by suggested improvements. Same dancer, after receiving advice, repeats the three actions, accompanied this time by the percussion played by the partner. The responsibility for the timing is given to the partner with the percussion.

**6–8** Partners change over and the new dancer, after their experience as teacher-coach, should be able to present a good performance with neat actions, clear shapes, and good use of space and effort. Once again, the new dancers sit to be advised and helped by the observing partner, who is asked to 'Tell your partner something that you particularly liked and tell them one thing that might improve the performance' to help them as they perform again.

# Lesson Plan 6 • 30 minutes
## February

**Theme:** *Traditional dance.*

## Warm-up Activities
### 5 minutes

1 Partners, travel side by side, keeping in time with the music. One of you will decide your actions, which each take eight bars of the music. Try to include two or three different actions. A change of direction on '8' looks very attractive.

2 Other partner, can you decide on actions to take your pair apart and then bring you together again? Separate for eight counts, then come together again for eight counts.

3 Partners, practise a four-part repeating pattern of travelling side by side; parting; closing; travelling together.

## Teach a Dance — Djatchko Kolo (Yugoslavian Folk Dance)
### 20 minutes

**Music:** *Djatchko Kolo*, Society for International Folk Dancing (cassette and book 3)

**Formation:** An open circle with teacher at right hand open end. This simple dance can be learned easily, with the teacher calling out and demonstrating each movement straight away with the music, and the class copying the teacher.

**Figure 1**

| | | |
|---|---|---|
| Bar 1 | Beat 1 | Step right foot to right. |
| | 2 | Close left foot to right foot. |
| | 3 | Step right foot to right. |
| | 4 | Swing left foot across right foot. |
| Bar 2 | Beats 1–4 | Repeat Bar 1 to the left, starting with left foot. |
| Bars 3 and 4 | | Repeat all of above. |

**Figure 2**

| | | |
|---|---|---|
| Bar 5 | Beat 1 | Step right foot to right. |
| | 2 | Swing left foot across right foot. |
| | 3 | Step left foot to left. |
| | 4 | Swing right foot across left foot. |
| Bar 6 | Beats 1–4 | Repeat Bar 5. |

**Figure 3**

| | |
|---|---|
| Bars 7 and 8 | Starting with right foot, perform seven little walking steps to right and point heel of left foot on the floor on '8'. |
| Bars 9 and 10 | Seven steps to left and point heel of right foot on the floor on '8'. |

Keep repeating dance from beginning.

## Revise a Favourite Dance
### 5 minutes

Ideally, this favourite dance, often chosen by the pupils, will contrast with the new dance of this lesson. It could be a revision of January's 'Winter' Dance.

**Dance**

# Teaching notes and NC guidance
## Development over 4 lessons

Pupils should be taught to perform movements or patterns, including some from existing dance traditions. Pupils should be able to show control in linking actions together.

A traditional Dance lesson has many attractions. The warm-up gives the lesson a lively, repeating, rhythmic start, always with the possibility of development into enjoyable partner activity. The four-part repeating pattern gives the opportunity for varied, creative activity, which is a good balance to the formal steps and figures of the folk dance.

When the steps and patterns of the dance are easy, as here, pupils quickly gain the pleasure of learning, mastering, repeating and improving another dance to add to their expanding repertoire. The circle formation lends itself to all pupils being able to see and copy the teacher's lead from start to finish. The slow rhythm at the start of the dance, accompanied by the teacher's rhythmic accompaniment of the simple actions, provides an almost instantly learned dance. Improvement comes with repetitions of the dance, with a different emphasis each time. 'Keep the circle round; grip with hands higher than elbows; erect posture throughout; neat steps and swings.'

## Warm-up Activities

1   An instant start with number one partner showing the two or three simple actions being repeated in time with the eight-count pattern of the music. The suggested change of direction will be helpful anyway as partners approach a wall or other couples.

2   Number two partner is challenged to plan actions suitable for parting and closing, taking eight counts for each. Cross-over steps and a step-close chasse are neat and do not take up too much space.

3   'Showing control in linking actions' is the challenge. 'Can you show me your joined-up, four-part sequence of joined-up travelling actions; joined-up parting and closing actions; and joined-up travelling together?'

## Teach a Dance – Djatchko Kolo (Yugoslavian Folk Dance)

The combination of very slow music, simple steps and a teacher in the circle demonstrating each figure makes this an easy dance to teach. The teacher's accompanying commentary for the first figure 'Step right, close left, step right, swing left; step left, close right, step left, swing right' is easy to understand and follow and is helped by the whole circle and the teacher moving in the correct directions.

Figures 2 and 3 are equally simple to learn and follow; repetition helps to reinforce the learning.

## Revise a Favourite Dance

Ease of learning and a successful double performance of the lesson's dance usually leaves enough time for a competent, enthusiastic class to be told, 'Well done. You worked really well and did that new dance brilliantly. Would anyone like to suggest a different dance for us to finish with? A more lively dance, not in a circle, and one that you yourselves created might be a good contrast.'

# Lesson Plan 7 • 30 minutes
## March

**Theme:** *Creating simple characters in response to music.*

## Warm-up Activities
### 5 minutes

1 Let's warm up with some actions that might describe different types of people. Off we go, proud soldiers. March, march, swing your arms; left, right, left, right; lift your knees, lift your arms; 1, 2, 3, 4.

2 Well done, proud soldiers. Ready again? Dithery person, here and there; ooops, I don't know where I'm going; side to side, forwards and back; turn around, change my mind.

3 Well dithered! One more. Ready? Tired person, flop about; dangling arms and heavy head; dragging legs and sagging knees.

## Movement Skills Training
### 15 minutes

1 Listen to the slow, swaggering rhythm of the music. Feel the 1, 2, 3, 4 repeating beat and imagine yourself as someone very important, stepping out confidently to it.

2 Let's try some proud, slow steps, just like a very self-confident policeman or policewoman might do. Go!

3 Well done. This time, pretend you are on your beat, patrolling the streets where you live. Turn corners; cross roads, looking right, left, right; and let your cocky head and shoulders say 'All's well. We don't have any baddies around here.'

4 That was excellent. You all look very cocky and proud. Now let's try some suspicious 'Baddie' movements as if you are sneaking along behind one of these very special coppers, silently keeping just out of sight. Use little runs, dodging behind bushes, letter boxes, in driveways or in doorways. Off you go!

5 Sometimes you will be close behind, copying the swaggering, cocky walking – and being a little bit cocky yourself. You can stop and start together; sometimes freeze while the copper looks around; even pretend to be simply reading a paper or looking at your watch. Let's pretend to be self-confident baddies. Go!

## Dance — Cops and Robbers
### 10 minutes

**Music: The 'Pink Panther' theme from** *The Pink Panther* **by Henry Mancini and his Orchestra (ND80832)**

1 Find a partner and decide who is the copper and who is the robber. Stand ready for our practice, our little game of chase. Let's see if the cops can do a repeating pattern of travelling so that the baddie can also repeat his or her pattern of secret following, weaving in and out, behind, side to side, close-up copying and freezing still. Start with the music.

2 Well done, cocky cops and robbers. This time I will stop the music as a signal for the copper to turn suddenly and catch the baddie. Running away is not allowed, you baddies! The goodies will grab hold with one hand and hold their truncheons above their partner's head with the other hand, expressing 'Gotcha!' The poor loser will express 'It's a fair cop, officer'. Ready? Go! (Let pupils perform for about one minute, then the music is suddenly stopped.)

3 Hold your positions, please. Well done. Now relax and we'll look at each half of the class in turn to see the many brilliant ideas you have created. You can tell me which ones you like.

**Dance**

# Teaching notes and NC guidance
# Development over 4 lessons

Pupils should be taught to express and communicate moods, ideas and feelings, and develop their responses to music.

The 'feelings' referred to include the interesting contrast in the movement expressions of the confident, self-assured, slightly arrogant, swaggering policeman or policewoman, and the movement expressions of the equally cocky, self-assured, sometimes cheeky robber.

Pupils practise each of the two parts separately, sometimes adding individual, funny mannerisms to their big swaggering walkabout. A standing cop shines the toes on the back of the other trouser leg; sticks thumbs through the braces; twirls the baton; waves to the adoring public; occasionally looks bored at such a crime-free existence.

The pursuing robber, bursting with self-assurance, zigzags along, out of sight and out of hearing of the copper, sometimes hiding, then rushing after him or her. Occasionally, the cockiness leads to a close shadowing, mimicking the copper's every move. Both use larger than life, big body movements to express how pleased they are with themselves.

## Warm-up Activities

The use of imagery, with pupils pretending and imagining that they are moving like certain kinds of people, makes it easier to express pride, ditheriness or tiredness. Trying to express such feelings, in isolation, without reference to persons of those types, is much harder.

## Movement Skills Training

1   The music invites a shoulder-swaggering, high-stepping, arm-swinging walk, 'expressing moods and feelings' as the class imagines that they are brilliant, or are suddenly transformed into some VIP, arrogantly looking from side to side, to check that all are admiring them.

2–3 Along with their proud, slow steps, the coppers are asked to try to plan and add some other copper-like actions of their own. These gestures all need to be shared and admired. The bored yawns and the looks at the wristwatch all infer 'There's no baddies around here. We've cleaned up the area.'

4–5 Pupils are challenged to plan where the baddies will go, keeping out of sight, as they pursue their copper. 'Expressing ideas' includes ways to look innocent when the copper turns around.

## Cops and Robbers Dance

1–3 Couples are given the difficult challenge of planning and repeating the pathways followed in travelling and pursuing. A pattern of three or four proud, cop-like actions along a repeating route with the robber's repeated pattern of zigzagging from tree to doorway; dropping down low out of sight; close behind mimicking; and a quick-thinking innocent gesture, for example, will give observers plenty to 'look out for and tell me what you liked' during the demonstrations later. The music is stopped as the signal for the copper to apprehend the robber. Each then expresses the appropriate feelings after victory and defeat.

# Lesson Plan 8 • 30 minutes
## April

**Theme:** *Clowns.*

## Warm-up Activities
### 5 minutes

1   Let's try a warm-up that I call '8:4:2' and see if you can keep up with me. Eight skips forwards... go! Skip, 2, 3, 4, 5, 6, 7, stop!

2   Good. You all started and stopped with me. Now an easy four steps backwards... go! Step, 2, 3 and stop!

3   We've gone forwards. We've gone backwards. What direction do you think we will go next? Yes, sideways with two chasse steps. Do it slowly with me. Step to the side; close feet together; step to the side; close feet together. Now do it a little bit quicker. Side step, close; side step, close. Well done. Now let's try the whole of our '8:4:2'. Skip forwards, 3, 4, 5, 6, 7, 8; step backwards, 3, 4; side step, close, side step, close. Excellent. Again... go!

## Movement Skills Training
### 15 minutes

1   In our last lesson we thought about and moved like several different sorts of people – soldiers, ditherers, tired people and cops and robbers. At Easter time, as at Christmas time, there are often circuses to visit. What do you call the funny performers in a circus? Yes, clowns.

2   Show me a funny clown walk, please. Can you turn your toes in a long way, swing your arms across your chest, and swing your shoulders up and down a long way?

3   You might try your funny walk going backwards and sideways as well as forwards. Four steps each way would be a nice pattern.

4   Try a funny walk on your heels, or your toes, or one of each. Add lots of funny, big, swinging arm, shoulder and head movements.

5   Clowns do lots of balancing on one foot and then suddenly stumble, nearly falling down as they do little running steps to save themselves. Show me your funny balance shapes and your wobbling, stumbling quick steps to balance still again.

6   Sometimes they do lose balance and sit down on their bottom. Show me a balance on your bottom with legs stuck up in the air.

7   Now twist over on to your tummy and show me another funny balance, with arms and legs lifted and doing swimming actions.

## Dance — The Clowns
### 10 minutes

### Music: TV Sport from *Festival of Music* by Central Band of the R.A.F.

1   Practise a pattern of funny walks, funny balances, staggers and runs to save yourself, and funny stumbles into a balance on your bottom or chest, or one of each. Then jump up like 'Jack In The Box'.

2   Find a partner and pretend your partner needs cheering up. Find a good space for your little circus ring. One of you sit down as a spectator. The other one does his or her clown dance to include some funny walking, funny balancing, wobbling, staggering, and then a sit down and funny balance on your bottom or front, or both.

3   Well done. Have one more practice. You can use our 8:4:2 pattern if you like – eight funny walks, four funny balances, wobbles and staggering about, and two balances, one on seat and one on chest.

4   Hands up all the spectators who laughed because you were amused? Can anyone tell me what you thought was good fun?

5   Change over now to a new clown and a new spectator. Start when you are ready. Clowns, dancers, give us a good laugh, please.

**Dance**

# Teaching notes and NC guidance
## Development over 4 lessons

Pupils should be able to show that they can improve performance, through practice, alone and with a partner.

From performing the movement characteristics of hyper-confident cops and robbers, we move on to show the equally exaggerated typical movements of a circus clown. The eventual performance by the clown has far greater potential for variety and interest, and for a repeating pattern of funny movements. The funny walking in all directions on all parts of the feet, the unstable, wobbly balancing on feet, the staggering run to regain balance, and the falling to balance on seat or back can all be fitted into a repeating, contrasting pattern that aids remembering and improvement.

Partners' observations and comments also aid the altering, adapting and extending that promote further planning and an improved performance.

## Warm-up Activities

This individual, three-part, repeating and reducing sequence will keep pupils concentrating to remember: (a) the three different actions – skips, steps and chasse steps; (b) the three different directions – forwards, backwards and sideways; and (c) the three different lengths of the phrases – eight skips, four steps and two chasse steps.

## Movement Skills Training

After the experience gained in expressing, through body movements, the personality, feelings and moods of cops and robbers in the previous lesson, moving as a clown and expressing the feelings and personalities of clowns should be easier to achieve in this lesson. After the 'Show me a funny clown walk, please,' the teacher is at his or her busiest in the middle part of the lesson, questioning, challenging, encouraging, as well as giving direct advice and suggestions for improvement. Good demonstrations showing ideal outcomes and responses will be a regular feature within the 'training' part of the lesson. Pupils remember what they see and the important elements within movement – shapes, directions, effort – will be more clearly understood through demonstrations than through explanations alone.

## Clown Dance

1   The many separate features of clown-like actions – funny walks and balances, staggers, stumbles and balances on bottom or chest – all practised, repeated and improved in the middle of the lesson, are here linked into a four-part sequence.

2–5 Performing for your own partner in the typical performer and spectator setting of a small circus ring is a different, new and challenging experience for partners, requiring larger-than-life actions to make them realistic. Clowns need to perform strongly to be seen by spectators in the very back of the rows of seats. The 8:4:2 pattern of the start of the lesson is a good guide for a satisfactory length of performance in the created dance climax of the end of the lesson.

# Lesson Plan 9 • 30 minutes
## May

**Theme:** *Kittens.*

## Warm-up Activities
### 5 minutes

1 Lots of baby animals are born in spring and they have to learn how to use their muscles to move.

2 With silent feet, weave in and out of one another, trying out the different ways your legs can travel. If you were a baby animal – lamb, puppy, kitten – you might try a little run and jump up.

3 Run a little way, jump high, then bend down towards the ground for a silent landing. Jump up and do a bendy, squashy landing. A baby animal doesn't want to hurt its bones and lands gently.

4 Often the baby animal springs up, twists in the air, and lands facing another way. Try a jump, twist and gentle landing.

## Movement Skills Training
### 15 minutes

1 Let's think about how a kitten might try out its muscles. Lie curled up small on the carpet in your home. Can you roll over from one side of your body to the other side? Roll and roll; a curled-up roll; side to side; roll and roll. Well done, kittens.

2 Now sit up tall, and stretch out your body. Stretch up one paw, 1–4; pull it down, 5–8; stretch up the other paw, 1–4; pull it down, 5–8; stretch up both paws at the same time and this time try out your claws, 1–4; pull in your claws and paws, 5–8.

3 On hands and knees, try a whole-body stretch and arch up high, 1–4; relax down again, 5–8; whole body arch high, 1–4; relax down again, 5–8.

4 Jump up from your carpet. Go out into your garden and try a run and a jump, landing gently. Not a sound! Do it two or three times and you can try a clever twist to land facing a different way.

5 Here's a high fence. Run and jump high to balance and walk along it, forwards then backwards, forwards then backwards.

6 Be clever and balance on one foot only on the fence, stretching out all parts of your body. Balance again, on the other foot.

7 It's time to go indoors. Jump down from your high fence and do a soft, squashy landing. Go back to your carpet starting places.

## Dance – Kittens
### 10 minutes

1 All lie curled up small on your nice soft carpet. Roll over from one side of your body to the other side. Roll and roll.

2 Sit up tall and straight and try out one paw as you stretch, 2, 3, 4; pull in, 2, 3, 4; other paw, stretch, 2, 3, 4; pull in, 2, 3, 4; both paws and claws, stretch, 2, 3, 4; pull in, 2, 3, 4.

3 On your hands and knees, try out your whole body arching up... and down... and arch high up... and relax down.

4 Jump up and go out into the garden for a run and jump and a soft landing. Run, jump, land. Run, jump and twist and land. Now a really high jump up on to the fence.

5 Balance-walk slowly forwards, backwards, forwards, backwards. Now on one foot only, stretch everything. On to the other foot and a big stretch of your whole body. Really stretch.

6 Jump down very gently and walk back to your nice soft carpet.

7 Repetition; performance; comments; improved practice.

**Dance**

LIVERPOOL JOHN MOORES UNIVERSITY
LEARNING & INFORMATION SERVICES

# Teaching notes and NC guidance
# Development over 4 lessons

Pupils should be taught to adopt the best possible posture and use of the body as they perform imaginatively. Pupils should be able to show control in linking actions together.

The body's posture and use are more evident during whole-body movements such as bending, stretching, twisting, turning and arching than when we do the everyday actions of travelling using our legs. These whole-body movements are also performed slowly, which means that they can be performed thoughtfully and to the limits of the joints concerned.

In the 'Kittens' dance, movements are used to express the typical movement characteristics of a young animal recently born in Spring. Pupils are asked to be conscious of their posture and to be aware of the repeating patterns of joined-up movements as an aid to remembering, repeating and improving the dance with all its contrasts of action and use of space.

## Warm-up Activities

**1–2** Throughout the lesson, imagery helps our aim of learning and imagining how young baby animals learn to use their muscles to move, soon after their birth in Spring. The little run and jump and the uncertain, hither-and-thither travelling, are typical of young kittens and lambs.

**3–4** The soft and careful use of feet and legs in running is repeated in the jumps and squashy landings, protecting young bones and joints. A teacher demonstration, starting facing one end of the hall, then running and jumping to turn in the air, landing to face the other end of the hall, is a popular challenge.

## Movement Skills Training

**1** The 'Let's think about how a kitten might try out its muscles' start to the training part of the lesson puts the class 'in the picture' straight away and focuses their attention on the movements concerned. A teacher demonstration of the side-to-side rolls will show the hands clasped under the bent knees to make the whole spine rounded from shoulders to seat.

**2** Sitting tall after being curled, pupils slowly stretch and feel the paws reaching up and down, followed by the dual action of paws and claws.

**3** The strong arch high on hands and feet alternates with the whole body lowering without touching the floor. This is a strong exercise, arching or bridging, on hands and feet only.

**4–6** The run and jump in the garden can include the jump and turn with a squashy landing of the warm-up. The run and jump high on to the garden fence is followed by a slow, careful balance-walk forwards and backwards, with four steps each way, then repeated. At the end of each forwards and back travel, pupils are asked, 'Can you be a clever kitten and stand on one paw only on your fence?' The class, like the teacher, will discover that they have one leg that is better and more reliable for balancing on.

**7** The jump down from the fence needs to be done softly and with a nice, squashy landing on to the young feet and legs of our kittens, before they return to their own starting places.

## Kittens Dance

After the stage-by-stage teaching of the middle part of the lesson, pupils now dance the whole dance, guided and reminded by the teacher's demonstrations and commentary.

# Lesson Plan 10 • 30 minutes
## June

**Theme:** *Traditional dance.*

## Warm-up Activities
### 5 minutes

1  Join hands with your partner in a big circle. Stand, side by side, all facing anti-clockwise.

2  Travel around in the circle with eight skipping steps.

3  Face your partner, without touching, and do four setting steps. (Step to right, close left to right, step on right; Step to left, close right to left, step on left.) 1... 2, 3; 2... 2, 3; right... 2, 3; left... 2, 3.

4  Change places with your partner, holding hands for four counts.

5  Face your partner again and do four setting steps on the spot.

6  Change places with your partner, holding hands for four counts.

7  Perform eight skipping steps forwards, dancing side by side, hands joined.

8  Keep repeating this 32-count (4 × 8-count) pattern.

## Teach a Dance — Pat-A-Cake Polka (English Folk dance)
### 20 minutes

**Music:** *Pat-A-Cake Polka* by Blue Mountain Band (EFDS), from Community Dances Manual 1

**Formation:** A double circle with boys' backs to the centre. Directions given are those of the dancer on the inside of the circle.

**Figure A:** Boys, hold both of your partner's hands, facing sideways. Moving anti-clockwise, dance 'heel and toe' and two chasse steps to the boys' left. (Touch floor with leading heel, then toes, then the quick chasse action, left, right, left), and repeat back again to boys' right (leading heel and toe each time). Repeat the whole movement, using a good spring at the start of each movement. 'Heel, toe, chasse, 2, 3; heel, toe, 1, 2, 3.'

**Figure B:** Partners clap right hands together three times. Partners clap left hands together three times. Partners clap both hands together three times. Partners clap own knees three times.

**Figure C:** Boy turns partner around for four counts to the starting position to repeat the dance, or does a quick two-count turn followed by boy moving on one place, anti-clockwise, to make the dance progressive, dancing next with a new partner.

Repeat.

## Revise a Favourite Dance
### 5 minutes

To provide the variety and contrast which is always an attractive feature of a Dance lesson, it is recommended that this dance is not danced in a circle formation. Ideally, also, it will be one of a more modern, creative, less traditional type.

**Dance**

# Teaching notes and NC guidance
# Development over 4 lessons

Pupils should be taught to perform movements or patterns, including some from existing dance traditions and different times and cultures. Pupils should be able to show control in linking actions together in ways that suit the activities.

The dance has an A:B:C repeating pattern of movement actions that are linked together. 'A' is the chasse left and right, twice, 'B' is the quick hand-clapping and 'C' is the turning with your partner, back to your own place, ready to start again'. The NC required patterns of movement and the linking of actions together are both well represented in this, as in all traditional dances.

Because of the high speed of this dance, it is essential that the teacher vocally accompanies the actions, phrase by phrase, as a reminder to the pupils, especially focussing on their high speed. 'Heel, toe, side, 2, 3; heel, toe, side, 2, 3; heel, toe, chasse left; heel, toe, chasse right' and (clapping) 'Right, 2, 3; left, 2, 3; both, 2, 3; knees', both of which will be helped further by the teacher joining in with the actions.

## Warm-up Activities

1   In a side-by-side, hands-held position, hands should be held above bent-elbows height.

2   In the anti-clockwise skipping, pupils are asked to 'Keep your nice big circle shape.'

3–6 Setting on the spot and changing places, hands held, then setting again on the spot and changing places again, hands held, is quite difficult. If pupils have not been taught the setting step, a quick right, left, right; left, right, left stepping on the spot will suffice. In turning, hands are again held above bent-elbow height, with the pupil whose hands are underneath doing the guiding.

7   The dance ends as it started with eight anti-clockwise travelling steps with partners' hands joined.

## Teach a Dance – Pat-A-Cake-Polka (English Country Dance)

**Figure A:** In the double circle of couples with hands joined, the pupils with their backs to the centre are told that they are dancing the boys' part – even if pairs of boys and pairs of girls are in the habit of dancing together. The teacher explains that he or she is speaking to the pupil dancing the boys' part because a direction applying to that dancer is involved. The 'Heel, toe, chasse left; heel toe, chasse right', taught slowly without any music at this stage, will, of course, be the opposite direction for the ones in the outer circle. The pupil dancing the boy's part, with back to centre, guides his or her partner in the right direction with hands held above bent-elbow height, and with guiding partner's hands underneath, taking the weight. Movement is repeated

**Figure B:** Still without music while learning the dance, the teacher and a partner demonstrate the rapid clapping of 'Right, 2, 3; left, 2, 3; both, 2, 3; own knees, 2, 3.' All practise to the teacher's commentary reminder.

**Figure C:** The four-count turn, using two hands to help each other, is slow and easy, and the teacher needs to emphasise that there is plenty of time to complete the turn.

Dance is repeated, with music, accompanied by the teacher's continuous reminder/commentary.

# Lesson Plan 11 • 30 minutes
## July

**Theme:** *Friendships.*

## Warm-up Activities
### 5 minutes

1   Let's remind ourselves of the friendly way we joined hands and sang when you started school:

   *Let's join hands in one big ring,*
   *Let's join hands and let us sing,*
   *Let's join hands, both high and low,*
   *Let's drop hands and wave 'Hello!'*

2   Now let's skip to this jazzy music for eight counts, change direction and go off again. Skip, 2, 3, 4, 5, 6, change direction; skip, 2, 3, 4, 5, 6, change again; skip, 2, 3, 4, 5, 6, 7, stop!

3   Now, meet and give a friendly touch to some- one coming towards you, saying 'Hello! Hello!' Ready? Skip, 2, 3, 4, 5, 6, change direction; skip, 2, 3, 4, 5, meet and 'Hello! Hello!' – keep going!

## Movement Skills Training
### 10 minutes

1   Think about the time you started school, not knowing anyone in your class. Show me how you might have walked, skipped or run around the playground, all by yourself.

2   Walk in and out of one another, looking at those coming towards you. Show me a friendly smile, wave or nod your head as you pass them.

3   When I beat the drum, make a friendly contact with the nearest person: a handshake; friendly touch on the shoulder; flat hand to hand.

4   As you grew older you became good at playing with others. Find a partner, sit down and decide on a shared activity you enjoy. Dance together; throw and catch; walk.

## Dance – Friendships
### 15 minutes

1   Well done. Lots of good fun ideas. Can you now agree a three- or four-part pattern to make your sequence more interesting. Each of you suggest one or two ideas for your shared, repeating activity. Practise when you are ready.

2   Well done. Your repeating patterns improve each time. Remember them for later. Now go and stand by yourself for the start of our 'Friendships' dance, pretending it is your first day at school.

3   Playing all by yourselves, ready, begin! Find good spaces, well away from others. Be lively, please!

4   Change to walking in and out of others, looking at, smiling, waving or nodding your head.

5   On my drum beat, stop and make a friendly, gentle contact with the nearest person, then move on.

6   When my drum sounds twice, go to your partner and start your shared, enjoyable activity. Try to repeat and improve it.

7   Very well done. Let's look at each half of the class in turn, demonstrating the last part of the dance. Tell me what you liked.

8   Thank you for your excellent performances and your friendly, helpful comments. Now, let's all join hands in a big, friendly circle and sing:

   *Let's join hands, getting all together,*
   *Let's join hands in a circle round,*
   *In we skip, good friends together,*
   *Clap our hands and turn around.*
   *Hands joined again, keeping close together,*
   *Skipping back out, off we go,*
   *Our joined-up hands swing high and low,*
   *Now we shake hands and say 'Hello!'*

**Dance**

# Teaching notes and NC guidance
# Development over 4 lessons

Pupils should be able to show that they are able to involve themselves in the continuous process of planning, performing and evaluating.

Ideally, they will be working harder for longer in almost non-stop action, displaying greater control and versatility. There should be an impression of confidence, enthusiasm and enjoyment as they stamp the work with their own personality.

## Warm-up Activities

1 The sociable 'togetherness' potential of good Physical Education lessons was evident in the 'Let's join hands and wave "Hello!"' of the very first lesson of the Reception Year programme. Since then, in Dance lessons, pupils will have joined hands in a friendly way hundreds of times.

2–3 After skipping for six counts and changing direction on counts 7 and 8, pupils now alternate skipping for six with a direction change on counts 7 and 8 and skipping for six and giving a friendly hand touch to someone on counts 7 and 8, with a 'Hello! Hello!'

## Movement Skills Training

1 In these four stages of infant-school social development, pupils start as shy individuals, walking, skipping, running or galloping alone at play time in the playground. No-one is making any form of communication with anyone else.

2 As a start to socialising, pupils now look at and make friendly, smiling gestures and waves as they pass others near to them. A nod of the head in someone's direction is always pleasant to give and to receive.

3 'When I sound the drum, can you stop and show me how you can make a friendly contact with the nearest person? Please try to surprise me with interesting and maybe unusual body parts making contact – always in a gentle and friendly way.' Teacher commentary and praise as they touch pleases the couples mentioned and helps the less creative with ideas.

4 Partners co-operate, planning their shared play activity, as they now do naturally every week. The profusion of shared activity possibilities, all of which will have been experienced, is a tribute to an excellent programme of physical education.

## Friendships Dance

1–2 Partners are challenged to make the final sequences of their Dance programme's final lesson more interesting. Direction changes; being together and apart; some travelling and some dancing on the spot; strong body-shapes contrasts; and, of course, enthusiastic, vigorous and poised participation, are all elements being encouraged by the teacher.

3–6 Pupils now go to their places to dance: (a) the starting stage, dancing and playing alone as a new pupil; (b) the walking, looking at and smiling at others, second stage; (c) responding to a drum beat by making a gentle, friendly contact with someone; and, finally, (d) the partners' planned, shared, repeating pattern of friendly, enjoyable, playful activity.

7–9 Half-watching-half demonstrations with follow-up friendly comments from pupils and the teacher are followed by hands joined to move and sing 'in a big, friendly class circle'.

# Games

# Introduction to Games

Individual and team games are part of our national heritage and an essential part of the Physical Education programme. Skills learned during Games lessons easily lend themselves to being practised away from school, alone or with friends or parents, and are the skills most likely to be used in participating in worthwhile physical and sociable activities long after leaving school – an important, long-term aim in Physical Education.

Vigorous, whole-body activity in the fresh air promotes normal, healthy growth and physical development, stimulating the heart, lungs and big muscle groups, particularly the legs.

Games lessons come nearest of all Physical Education activities to demonstrating what we understand by the expression 'children at play'. Pupils are involved in play-like, exciting, adventurous chasing and dodging as they try to outwit opponents in games and competitive activities. Such close, friendly 'combat' with and against others can help to compensate for the increasingly isolated, over-protected, self-absorbed nature of much of today's childhood, with little healthy adventure.

Games are taught outdoors, in the fresh air, in the playground. For infant classes, the playground 'classroom' can be a netball court, if the school has one, or a rectangle, sub-divided into six or eight 8–10-metre rectangles.

The lesson starts with warming-up and footwork activities to improve stopping, starting, dodging, marking, running and jumping. Skills are taught individually and in pairs in the middle part of the lesson. During the course of a year a wide variety of games equipment will be experienced, ideally with the same equipment being used by all in the same lesson, so that teaching applies to all. In the most important, final part of the lesson, three different group practices or games provide an exciting and varied climax with near-continuous action for all.

The following monthly lesson plans and accompanying notes aim to provide teachers and schools with a wide variety of material for lesson content, development and progression. Each lesson is repeated three or four times to allow plenty of time for planning, practising and improving, which are essential elements in good practice in the National Curriculum.

# The playground Games 'classroom'

Infant-school Games lessons should be taught out of doors on the playground. Where no netball court is marked, the 'classroom' is a painted rectangle of six to eight 8–10-metre square grids.

This painted rectangle is essential because it:

a   contains the class in a limited space within which the teacher can see, manage and be easily seen and heard by the whole class, not needing to raise and strain his or her voice by shouting to be heard over great distances

b   gives the spaces needed for the three activities of the final group practices part of the lesson. Each space is normally two adjacent rectangles across the court. Where there are eight grids or small rectangles, two pairs can be used for any activity that benefits from extra space, such as short tennis

c   prevents accidents by keeping the class well away from any potential hazards such as concrete seats, hutted classrooms, fences or walls, all of which should be several metres outside the games rectangle

d   provides lines which are used in hundreds of ways during the infant years' Games programme. Pupils run and jump over; balance on; can be 'safe' on in chasing games; aim at; play net games over; use in limited-area 'invent a game or practice' situations; play end-to-end, two-with or two-against games; do side-to-side sprint relays.

With a new class each September, the teacher's main emphasis during a Games lesson on the playground is training the class to be aware of, and to remain within, the outside lines of the 'playground classroom' rectangle. 'Show me your best running as you go to all parts of our playground classroom. Visit the ends, sides, the middle and always keep inside the lines of our pretend classroom.'

## Games equipment

Teachers should ensure they have the following:

○   sets of 30 of: small balls; medium balls; large balls; beanbags; skipping ropes; playbats; hoops; short tennis rackets

○   10 × long, 24 ft (7 metre) skipping ropes for group skipping and for use as 'nets' for tennis and quoits

○   10 × rubber quoits

○   6 × 8 in (20 cm) foam balls

○ playground chalk

○ 1 × set Kwik Cricket

○ 8 × marker cones.

# Safe teaching of Games

A teacher's checklist of *safe practices* will include:

○ sensible, safe clothing with no watches, jewellery, rings, long trousers that catch heels or unbunched hair that impedes vision

○ good supervision by the teacher whose circulation, mainly on the outside looking in, means that the majority of the class can be seen at all times, with few behind the teacher's back

○ fast-moving, dodging and chasing children must be trained to remain inside the lines of the games rectangle

○ good behaviour with a tradition of quiet tongues and feet, and instant responses to instructions

○ an awareness by the class of danger points such as fences, walls, sheds, seats, or steps into buildings if a pupil has to leave the 'playground classroom' to recover a wandering ball

○ good teaching, which aims to develop skilful, well-controlled, safe movement, is a major contributor to safe practice

○ if there is strong sunshine, the teacher should face the sun when teaching or introducing a new activity, or when presenting a demonstration. The class will have the sun behind them, enabling them to see and understand more easily.

**Essential traditions,** when teaching, include:

1   Insisting on a safe, unselfish sharing of space; immediate responses to instructions, particularly the one to 'Stop!'; and a quiet atmosphere with pupils keen to improve. The class should understand they must be 'found working, not waiting' as their contribution to almost non-stop activity.

2   Inaction and 'lesson dead spots' must be avoided. These are caused by over-long explanations; too many stoppages for demonstrations followed by lengthy comments and discussion; and poor responses from a class who need to be asked to 'Stop!' too often.

3   While the thinking and planning, reflecting and evaluating requirements of the NC should always be a concern in teaching PE, the main emphasis must always be on the doing, the performing, the action.

4   The teacher's main aim should be a flowing, almost non-stop lesson with optimum activity. Children enjoy a lesson when 'it is fun; is exciting; has lots of action; all have a turn; you learn interesting new things; it makes you fitter; rules make it fair for everyone.'

**Planned aims,** as in all areas of Physical Education, include:

1   The promotion of normal, healthy growth and physical development.

2   The learning of skills to develop neat, skilful, well-controlled, versatile movement.

3   Helping pupils become good learners as well as good movers. Pupils are challenged to think for themselves and make decisions about their actions.

4   Developing pupils' self-confidence and self-esteem as achievements are recognised, praised and shared with others.

5   Developing desirable social qualities through friendly, co-operative, close relationships, which are an ever-present feature of these lessons.

6   Satisfying every pupil's entitlement to achieve physical competence in a broad and balanced Physical Education programme.

# How to teach a Games skill or practice

Excellent lesson 'pace' is expressed in almost non-stop activity with no bad behaviour stoppages and no 'dead spots' caused by long queues, over-long explanations or too many time-consuming demonstrations. The teaching of each of the skills which combine to make a Games lesson determines the quality of the lesson's pace – a main feature of an excellent Physical Education lesson.

A typical Games lesson, with its warm-up and footwork practices, skills practices and small-sided group practices and games, will include about a dozen skills. Whatever the skill, there is a pattern for teaching it:

1  **Quickly into action.** In a few words, explain the task and challenge the class to start. 'Can you stand, two big steps apart, and throw the small ball to your partner for a two-handed catch?' If a short demonstration is needed, then the teacher can work with a pupil who has been alerted. Class practice should start quickly after the five seconds it took the teacher to make the challenge.

2  **Emphasise the main teaching points, one at a time, while the class is working.** A well-behaved class does not need to be stopped to listen to the next point. 'Hold your hands forward to show your partner where to aim'; 'Watch the ball into your cupped hands.'

3  **Identify and praise good work, while class is working.** Comments are heard by all; remind the class of key points; and inspire the praised to even greater effort. 'Well done, Sarah and Daniel. You are throwing and catching at the right height and speed, and watching the ball into your hands.'

4  **Teach for individual improvement while class is working.** 'Patrick, hold both hands forward to give Christine a still target to aim at'; 'Ann and Alan, stand closer. You are far too far apart.'

5  **A demonstration can be used, briefly, to show good quality or an example of what is required.** 'Stop, everyone, please, and watch how Cara and Michael let their hands "give" as they receive the ball, to stop it bouncing out again.'

6  **Very occasionally (once, or twice at most in a lesson to avoid taking too much activity time) a short demonstration can be followed by comments.** 'Stop and watch Leroy and Emily. Tell me what makes their throwing and catching so smooth and accurate.' The class watch about six throws and three or four comments are invited. For example, 'They are nicely balanced with one foot forward'; 'Their hands are well forward, to take the ball early, then give, smoothly and gently.'

7  **Thanks are given to performers and those making helpful comments.** Further practice takes place with reminders of the good things seen and commented on. We remember what we see and pupils need to be given the opportunity to try some of the things seen and praised.

## Throwing and Catching Practices for Infants

Throwing and catching are the two most frequently used skills in primary school Games lessons where small balls, medium sized balls, beanbags and quoits can be used all year round.

### Individual practices

1  One hand to one hand.

2  One hand to both hands.

3  Two hands to two hands.

4  Throw up, clap, catch.

5  Little throw, catch; medium throw, catch; higher throw, catch.

6  Throw up and forwards a little way, run to catch.

7  Aim beanbag at nearby line or mark. Pick up, aim at new mark.

8  Walk, let ball bounce, catch with both hands.

9  Jog, throw and catch just in front of eyes with cupped hands.

10  Jog, throw and catch. On 'Change!' put ball down and find another.

## Partner practices

1 Walk side by side, handing the ball to partner's cupped hands.

2 Throw and catch, two metres apart, two hands to two hands.

3 One hand to throw, two to catch. Partner's hands well forwards.

4 Catch low, below knees; medium at waist; higher at head height.

5 Aim ball at a line between the two partners. Partner catches after bounce. Count hits on line.

6 Throw. Move one metre further apart. Throw. One or two more moves and throws, then back again to starting positions.

7 Walk, side by side, throwing just ahead of partner's hands.

8 Follow the leader who shows ways to throw and catch.

9 One throws straight to partner who bounces it back. Change after six.

10 Throw to partner. Move to a new space for return throw. 'Give and go!'

## Group practices and small-sided games

1 Aiming contest in twos to land beanbag in hoop, 2–3 metres away.

2 Aiming contest through high hoop held by partner. Best of three.

3 Walk, throwing and catching beanbag. From two metres away, aim to land it in one of the hoops. (Several scattered in the area.)

4 One partner stands still, the other jogs around for throw and catch.

5 Follow leader, throwing and catching, trying one- and two-handed ways to practise. Change and see if follower can remember them.

6 Beanbag each at a line, 3 metres apart. Aim at partner's line. Change places, pick up own bag and repeat.

7 Partners at long rope 'net'. How many throws over net without dropping beanbag? Throw with one hand to two hands reaching.

8 Beanbag among three. 'Piggy in the middle', with pairs trying to throw to each other, keeping beanbag away from one in the middle.

9 'Wandering ball' with three of the group outside the circle, passing the ball across to bypass and outwit the one in the circle.

10 Team passing, three against one, with the three passing close enough to receive catches but giving the one a chance.

11 Two versus two, or four versus four, end line touch with several agreed ways to score. For example, touch ball down on end line; bounce it in one of the hoops in the corners; pass to partner on end line.

# National Curriculum requirements for Games – Key Stage 1: the main features

'The Government believes that two hours of physical activity a week, including the National Curriculum for Physical Education and extra-curricular activities, should be an aspiration for all schools. This applies to all key stages.'

## Programme of Study

Pupils should be taught to:

a   travel with, send and receive a ball and other equipment in different ways. Equipment used in the following lessons includes balls of various sizes and textures, bats, rackets, beanbags, quoits, skipping ropes of different lengths, and hoops

b   develop these skills for simple net, striking/fielding and invasion-type games. Neat, controlled footwork with changes of speed and direction used to pursue, dodge or simply to give you ample practising room, makes chasing games more exciting and safe

c   play simple, competitive net, striking/fielding and invasion-type games that they and others have made, using simple tactics for attacking and defending. From the simplest 'Can you aim at the line between you and your partner and count your good hits to see who is the winner?' to 'Can you invent a simple, 1-against-1 game, using one ball and a part of a line, and using the skills we have just practised?' to 'Can your group of four make up a game, using the large ball and two of the lines around the area?'

At every stage, the pupils will be asked to consider, 'How will you score in your little game? What will be the main rule to make your game fair for everyone? How will your game re-start after a score? Can you think of any extra ways to make the game more exciting?' and, if necessary, 'How can we help to make scoring easier?' (e.g. defending team will be 'passive', not going for the ball).

## Attainment Target

Pupils should be able to demonstrate that they can:

a   select and use skills, actions and ideas appropriately, applying them with co-ordination and control (e.g. throw ball up, jump to catch it, land nicely poised)

b   vary, copy, repeat and link skills, actions and ideas in ways that suit the activities (i.e. ample equipment needed to provide an implement each to enable such practising)

c   talk about differences between own and others' work and suggest ways to improve their own performance

d   recognise and describe the changes that happen to the body during exercise (from increased warmth, perspiration, deep breathing, chest rising and falling, and fatigue, to 'feeling relaxed, calm, happy, good inside, proud, excited').

## Main NC Headings when considering assessment, progression and expectation

○   **Planning** – in a safe, thoughtful, focused way, thinking ahead to an intended outcome. The set criteria are used and there is evidence of originality and variety

○   **Performing and improving performance** – pupils work hard, concentrating on the main feature of the task, to present a neat, efficient, poised, confident performance, under control

○   **Linking actions** – pupils work harder for longer, smoothly and safely, using space sensibly, and able to remember and repeat the whole sequence successfully from its start right through to its controlled finish

○   **Reflecting and making judgements** to help pupils progress and improve, as they plan again adapting and altering as required, guided by their own and others' comments and judgements.

# Year 2 Games programme

Pupils should be able to:

| Autumn | Spring | Summer |
|---|---|---|
| 1 Respond readily and vigorously to instructions. | 1 Respond immediately and safely, showing a whole-hearted attitude in the pursuit of improved skill. | 1 Show improved ability in running, hurdling, and jumping high and long. |
| 2 Practise, almost non-stop, to improve. | 2 Plan and practise thoughtfully, almost without stopping – repeating, adapting, improving. | 2 Show good control in sending and receiving a ball, alone and with a partner – bat, bowl, throw, roll, serve. |
| 3 Show good space awareness, avoiding others, for continuous, safe, undisturbed practice. | 3 Link movements together with increasing versatility and control, using Games equipment with skill, confidence and enthusiasm. | 3 Continue practising with a wide range of implements – racket and ball, rope, hoop, beanbag, quoit. |
| 4 Run and jump strongly, with good, relaxed arm, leg and upper body carriage, tall and poised. | 4 Demonstrate knowledge and understanding as well as skill in well-planned performances. | 4 Practise hand and racket short tennis over a line or net co-operatively with a partner, and, when ready, competitively, agreeing how to serve, score and keep the game going. |
| 5 Play chasing and dodging games with good footwork, and changes of speed and direction. | 5 Show increasing awareness of ways to receive, send and travel with a ball. | 5 Invent a game in 2s or 4s, in a small area, deciding scoring systems, the main rules, and how to re-start after scoring. |
| 6 Plan to practise a variety of skills with ball, bat, beanbag, hoop, rope, quoit, racket. | 6 Make up and play simple games with little equipment and few, simple rules. | 6 Practise to improve skipping of all kinds, including follow a leader and group skipping with a long rope. |
| 7 Link movements with increasing control, keeping action going to work harder for longer. | 7 Work vigorously to keep warm. | 7 Play 1 v 1, 2 v 2, 3 v 1, 3 v 3, and 4 v 4 competitive games, depending on skill levels, of batting, bowling, fielding; serving, striking, returning. |
| 8 Co-operate with a partner to: send, receive and travel with a ball; rally over net with ball and quoit; lead and follow. | 8 Chase and dodge, changing speed and direction, to avoid being caught. | 8 Link series of simple actions – skip on spot and moving; throw, run, catch; run to field, pick up, throw in; throw to self, bat up, catch, jump high and long. |
| 9 Pass a big ball to partner, then move to a new space for the return pass. Give and go! | 9 Co-operate with a partner to improve skills with ball, beanbag, bat, rope. | 9 Display fair play, honest competition and good sporting behaviour. |
| 10 Play 3 v 1, with the '3' keeping ball from '1' by passing and moving to space for next pass. | 10 Play simple 1 v 1, 2 v 1, 3 v 1 and 2 v 2 games in a limited space, with simple rules and scoring systems. | 10 With partners and in groups, invent and play simple versions of well-known games like tennis and cricket. |
| 11 Make up and play simple games with e.g. one ball, two hoops and a limited area. Decide the main rules, how to score and how to re-start. | 11 Demonstrate skills willingly, and be keen to learn from and use helpful constructive comments made. | 11 Describe what you and others are doing, and make simple judgements on a peformance. |
| 12 Pick out the main features in a demonstration and praise them. | | |

# Lesson Plan 1 • 30 minutes
## September

**Emphasis on:** *re-establishing tradition of: (a) immediate responses to instructions; (b) enthusiastic and vigorous participation; (c) safe and sensible sharing of space.*

## Warm-up and Footwork Practices
### 5 minutes

1 Show me that you can run quietly, without following anyone. Lift heels, knees, arms and head, and run straight, not curving. (Unless taught otherwise, children run in an anti-clockwise circle.)

2 Can you use this best, straight running to visit every part of our playground 'classroom' within the four outer lines? Visit the ends, sides, corners and the middle sometimes.

3 When I call 'Stop!' show me how quickly you can respond and stand, balanced on tiptoes, on the nearest line, arms stretched sideways to help your balance.

## Skills Practices: with small bats and balls
### 10 minutes

### Individual practices

1 Walk around with ball balanced on bat, near eye level. Now change to gentle batting upwards using wrist action only. What is your best, new year score? Five or more is very good.

2 Throw ball straight up with one hand, let it bounce up, bat it up, catch it with one hand. Repeat.

3 Can you walk around, always looking for good spaces, batting your ball down on to the ground?

### Partner practices

1 Can you and your partner keep your ball up in the air between you, using gentle strokes by using your wrists only? (Not elbows or shoulders, which are far too powerful for this neat stroke.)

2 Can you strike the ball up to land between you for a return strike by your partner? Stand only two or three steps apart and keep your best score.

3 One partner bowls underarm with a very slow and low lob for partner to bat back to bowler for catching practice. Have six goes and then change.

## Group Practices
### 15 minutes

### Large ball between two

Practise ways to send the ball to your partner, both standing and on the move. How many body parts can send ball quite accurately?

### Fours: one bat and ball; half the area

Can you make up a simple batting game, using bat, ball, skittles and lines to 'contain' games? How will you score? How will you be 'out'? How many balls each?

### Skipping rope each

Free practice to revise and try out some of the many ways of skipping. On the spot, feet apart or together, or one after the other. Moving in different directions.

# Teaching notes and NC guidance
# Development over 4 lessons

## Warm-up and Footwork Practices

1  Class needs a start-of-year reminder of what 'good running' means or they will return to the noisy, anti-clockwise running in one big circle, typical of much primary school running.

2  Running along straight lines, not curves, enables pupils to visit every part of the teaching space because they are continually coming to an outside line and needing to change direction. Such 'non following' in physical education gives each child lots of room and time to perform unimpeded.

3  Exercises in listening and responding immediately to the teacher's signals and instructions are important. Poor responders can be made to behave and respond better so that valuable time is not wasted waiting for someone each time.

## Skills Practices: with small bats and balls

### Individual practices

1  'Performing simple skills safely to join them together with increasing control' satisfies a main requirement within the NC. Balancing, alternate with a little hit upwards, watching the ball closely and using just the right amount of force, is a difficult skill for young pupils.

2  Batting the ball almost straight upwards to let it bounce almost straight upwards for the next hit needs a gentle touch, using a wrist action, not elbow or shoulder.

3  Using the bat like a big hand, pupils now hit the ball down and a little way forwards as they walk forwards, trying to make the bounce up come nicely to where the next step will take them.

### Partner practices

1  Standing next to each other, each partner in turn bats the ball straight up between them. The other partner makes the next little hit up. Pupils have to be told to stand 'close enough to touch your partner' so that a vertical (and very gentle) hit is possible.

2  Still close together, they hit the ball gently and straight up, high enough to make it bounce up for the partner to hit up.

3  At 3 metres apart, the bowler aims a 'low and slow' lob to land about 1 metre ahead of the batter to bounce up for a hit at chest height, ideally side-on to the bowler and catcher.

## Group practices

### Large ball between two

A variety of ways to send (including throwing), receive and travel with a ball is an NC emphasis. The ways pupils receive and control are as important as the sending.

### Fours: one bat and ball; half the area

In half of their third of the teaching area, pupils are challenged to 'invent a simple batting game'. They must agree on the style of the game, how to score, how to involve all in the game fairly, and the one main rule that keeps the game going and fair.

### Skipping rope each

Free practice will be as varied and challenging as teacher commentary and praise can make it. Quiet, neat footwork; good rope control; and varied directions and speeds are encouraged.

# Lesson Plan 2 • 30 minutes
## October

**Emphasis on:** *(a) practising, almost non-stop, to improve; (b) practising good footwork, including dodging and chasing; (c) practising varied ball skills.*

## Warm-up and Footwork Practices
### 5 minutes

1  Run, practising little side steps to avoid others coming towards you. In a side step, one foot goes out to the side instead of forwards, to put you on to a new line, still facing the same way.

2  Five points tag. All have five points to start with. When touched you lose one of your points. (N.B. No dangerous pushing. Touch gently.)

## Skills Practices: with a large or medium ball
### 10 minutes

### Individual practices

1  Walk, throwing the ball just above your head and then catching it. Keep your fingers spread, thumbs back, fingers around the sides of the ball.

2  Bounce the ball using your finger-tips, left and right hands, on the spot, and weaving in and out of the others.

3  Dribble the ball like a footballer, keeping it close. When I call 'Stop!' see how quickly you can control the ball by placing a foot on top of the ball, to make it still.

### Partner practices

1  About 3 metres apart only, throw a two-handed pass to your partner and move sideways into a space for the return pass, still only 3 metres apart. Pass; move; receive.

2  Shadow dribbling, one ball. Leader shows partner favourite ways to dribble, using feet or hands. After six touches, change over and see if the follower can copy the routine exactly.

## Group Practices
### 15 minutes

### Quoits: with a partner; 1 v 1

Long rope 'net' tied between chairs. Play quoits and try to score by landing quoit on a partner's side for a point. Decide how to start, how many points to a game, and any other rules to help the game.

### Large ball among four: 3 v 1

'Wandering ball' with three of group on outside of big chalk circle passing the ball across the circle, bypassing and outwitting the one in the circle. Keep changing one in centre who works hard to intercept the ball.

### Partners: with a hoop each

Stand at opposite side of court from partner. Bowl hoop to pass each other and go to partner's line. Keep close to and in control of your hoop. Now can you show me another good partner practice you like?

# Teaching notes and NC guidance
# Development over 4 lessons

## Warm-up and Footwork Practices

1 To give continuous practice of meeting others, the side step is done in one third of the teaching space, to bring everyone close together. The running is at half speed to let pupils focus on and do the side steps in safety.

2 In five points tag, the class is asked to dodge away from chasers, not race away at high speed. 'Dodging' means changing direction; side stepping; and making sudden changes of speed, including stopping suddenly. The game is stopped every 16 seconds to let the teacher check on 'Who were the best dodgers with 5 points still? Who were the best chasers, catching 3 or more?'

## Skills Practices: with a large or medium ball

### Individual practices

1 The throw to above the head is performed from a high position at head height with the ball in both hands, arms slightly bent, and fingers pointing upwards. Hands receive with a little 'give' each time, and eyes watch the ball closely.

2 In bouncing, basketball fashion, we use the fingertips and a wrist action, up and down where you stand, and forwards and down when travelling. Use left and right hands to avoid others coming towards you.

### Partner practices

1 The two-handed chest pass starts in front of the passer's chest with hands higher than elbows. Ball is pushed to partner's chest height for a catch where the arms 'give' to stop ball rebounding away. The move sideways to a new space to receive the next pass is one of the most important moves in invasion games. 'Pass, then move!' will continually be said during games lessons from now on. This movement is needed by a team to advance itself and the ball towards the opponents' goal line.

2 Shadow dribbling trains the leader to think about and plan a short sequence, and trains the follower to observe and be able to repeat the sequence.

## Group Practices

### Quoits: with a partner; 1 v 1

In competitive, 1-against-1 quoits, the 'net' is a long rope tied between chairs or higher objects, ideally at chest height so that the throw has to be high enough to 'let the quoit see over the net'. A point is scored if the quoit lands on the ground. Pairs have to agree how to start or serve; ways to score; and one main rule designed to keep the game going and fair.

### Large ball among four: 3 v 1

In 'wandering ball' or piggy in the middle around a chalk circle of 2 metres diameter, the 3 must stay outside the circle, and the 1 must stay inside it. If the game keeps breaking down with few passes being made, the 1 can be asked to be passive, keeping arms by the sides, to make passing easier.

### Partners: with a hoop each

Bowling the hoops to change places, line to line, is done at a walking pace, keeping beside your hoop, not pushing it far ahead.

# Lesson Plan 3 • 30 minutes
## November

**Emphasis on:** *(a) linking movements with increasing control to keep the action going longer; (b) making up and playing simple games.*

## Warm-up and Footwork Practices
### 5 minutes

1 Change between easy jogging and bursts of sprinting. Jog when you are near others. Sprint when you see a good space. Arms and heels are low in jogging, lifted up when sprinting.

2 Chain tag with four couples starting off as chasers. When someone is caught, he or she joins the pair that caught them. When the chain grows to four, it separates into two chains of one couple each who then continue to chase. Winner is last one caught.

## Skills Practices: with a skipping rope
### 10 minutes

### Individual practices

1 Practise the slow overhead pull and the easy step over as the rope slides along the ground towards you. Hand action is very small.

2 Now skip on the move with a sort of running action. Which is your leading leg?

### Partner practices

Stand where you can see each other easily. A will skip for about six travelling counts and stop. B will skip for about six counts and stop. Can you include a variety of directions and try to have one of the pair on the move at all times? Your working–resting partner skipping will be interesting if you can do some opposites (e.g. forwards, backwards; feet apart, together).

## Group Practices
### 15 minutes

### Large ball among four: 2 v 2

Play 2 against 2 in half of your area, and score by bouncing ball in one of the choice of hoops. Can you agree one main rule to help keep the game fair? What other way to score can you think of to give more goals?

### Long skipping rope among four

Two swing rope low, for others to jump. While learning, do not swing the long rope overhead. Come in to the rope when it is swinging away from you. Leave the rope left when it is swinging to the right.

### Beanbag among three: 2 v 1

Piggy in the middle with the two with the beanbag moving to a space to receive from partner. Middle person tries to intercept by spreading arms and legs wide. Use two-handed pass, then move to a new space, ready.

**Games**

# Teaching notes and NC guidance
# Development over 4 lessons

## Warm-up and Footwork Practices

1   The teacher can demonstrate easy jogging with arms and heels lower than normal, lively running, an upright body, and with a nice, steady rhythm. Short bursts of sprinting for 4 to 6 metres through a space has rapid short strides, a high lift of heels and knees, and a body inclined forwards.

2   In the chasing and dodging chain tag, chasers must touch gently and safely, and not push the dodgers to catch them. Encourage the dodgers to try side steps, direction changes and sudden changes of speed to evade chasers, never high speed running away.

## Skills Practices: with a skipping rope

### Individual practices

1   All practise the slow, overhead pull to remind themselves of the easy, wide hand action and the physically easy step over the rope.

2   The slow step over the rope becomes a quicker run over it as the class try to skip 'on the move', noting which leg is leading. This one foot after the other is easier, physically, than skipping on the spot with feet together. 'Easier' means you can keep going and keep warm as we move into colder weather.

### Partner practices

Resting and working; watching and doing; alternate skipping gives pupils a rest and challenges them to plan a sequence that has variety (and quality, we hope) of actions, leg shapes, directions and speeds. 'Someone working at all times' means a smooth transition from one performer to the partner, with excellent timing.

## Group Practices

### Large ball among 4: 2 v 2

The competitive, 2 versus 2, with one ball in half of their third, requires the passing pair to 'Pass, then move to a new space to receive the next pass' or they will never advance themselves or the ball, because you may not run carrying the ball. To make this feature succeed, it might be necessary to ask the two defenders to be passive, never going for the ball when it is being passed, but able to intercept shots.

### Long skipping rope among four

A 4-metres long rope is swung low, from side to side, vigorously. (Not overhead to start with.) Group has turns at swinging the rope, then trying to come in to skip. They should aim to come in to skip along the line on the ground where the rope touches each time. Beginners usually jump too early at a point where the rope is well off the ground.

### Beanbag among three: 2 v 1

The pair with the beanbag are asked to wait until the receiving partner has moved sideways into a space before throwing to that partner. They must not throw it over the head of the one in the middle. If this game is being badly done with few successful passes and catches, ask the one in the middle to be passive and not challenge for the beanbag.

# Lesson Plan 4 • 30 minutes
## December

**Emphasis on:** *(a) near-continuous, lively action to become and to stay warm; (b) strong leg activity, which increases winter warmth.*

## Warm-up and Footwork Practices
### 5 minutes

1   Follow the leader, where the leader uses a simple repeating pattern, e.g. walk 6, jog 6, jump with feet together for 6. Change over and see if follower can remember and repeat it all.

2   'Line safe tag', where the six chasers can catch you if you are not on a line, i.e. on a line is safe, untouchable. Those caught take a coloured band and become chasers. If dodgers are staying too long on their lines, teacher calls 'All move!'

## Skills Practices: with a beanbag
### 10 minutes

### Individual practices

1   Jog forwards, throwing up and forwards a little way with one hand, and catching with two hands.

2   Throw low (chest height), throw medium (head height), throw high (as high as can be caught reliably), and try to do this on the move to keep warm.

3   Stand. Throw beanbag to one side or the other; in front of you; or behind you. Can you move quickly to catch it with two hands? Throw it high enough to give you time to get there.

### Partner practices

1   Jog around, side by side, passing the bag like a rugby ball with long straight arms swinging across from side to side. Throw and catch with two hands. Aim just in front of your partner.

2   Stand 3 metres apart. Throw with one hand, move to a new space and catch with two hands. Hold your hands forwards to show your partner a target to aim at. Pass; move; receive, moving sideways and forwards to maintain the 2–3-metre distance.

3   Stand very close. Throw above partner's head for a high jump up to catch at full stretch with one or both hands.

## Group Practices
### 15 minutes

### Free practice: with choice of ropes, hoops, balls, quoits, bats and balls

Choose something you can use in a lively, vigorous way, using large body actions, as you share the space sensibly.

### Beanbag among four: team passing; 2 against 2, or 3 against 1

Play 2 v 2, if good skill level; 3 v 1 if not so good. Keep close enough to give partner an easy 2–3-metre pass. Three good passes can equal a goal.

### Partners with a large ball

Keep on the move to show me how you can carry, send and receive your ball with lots of success, keeping going, almost non-stop, to keep warm.

**Games**

# Teaching notes and NC guidance
# Development over 4 lessons

## Warm-up and Footwork Practices

1   To inspire an instant response, the class can be asked to follow the leader performing the teacher's suggested, simple, short sequence with its walk, jog and jump, always looking for good spaces to lead your partner through. When 'pattern' is understood the class can be invited to keep the same simple sequence or adapt it to one of their own planning. Each part must be kept short.

2   Because December can be very cold we do not want too many instances of inactive loitering on the 'safe' lines. After 20 seconds, the teacher checks on who were the best dodgers, still not caught, and changes the chasers over.

## Skills Practices: with a beanbag

### Individual practices

1   Because it is easy to catch and hold, a beanbag is a good implement for cold weather throwing and catching, as it does not roll or bounce away from you. The little throw forwards is to about head height and just ahead of you.

2   Still jogging while practising to keep warm, still throwing with one hand and catching with two, pupils feel the different amounts of force needed to make it go 'Low; medium; higher'.

3   A standing throw up and to one side or to the front is followed by a quick move to a position where you can catch the beanbag while standing still with hands forwards and cupped – another example of 'simple skills joined together'.

### Partner Practices

1   In jogging side by side, emphasise that your body is facing forwards normally with long, low arms swinging from side to side, with the hands around the sides of the ball. (Children often run with their whole body moving sideways, not facing to the front.)

2   This 'Pass, then move!' practice is one of the most important in Games. The move, usually to one side and forwards, into a space, means that you are available to receive the next pass in a space, and the ball is advancing towards the opponents' line.

3   Jumping partner must wait until ball starts to come down before he or she jumps up to meet it at full stretch, then land, nicely balanced, with feet astride.

## Group Practices

### Free practice: with a choice of ropes, hoops, balls, quoits, bats and balls

In free practice in December, the main feature must be the vigorous action asked for, to keep warm. Ideally, whole-body actions, able to be repeated, non-stop, are being planned and practised, e.g. running style skipping with high knee raising.

### Beanbag among four: team passing; 2 against 2, or 3 against 1

Competitive 2 v 2, or 3 v 1, team passing with a beanbag, gives excellent practice in the important 'Pass, then move for the next pass – in a space you have made by moving.'

### Partners with a large ball

The three-part sequence asks for a controlled carry, a sending that is accurate and neat, and a receiving that looks easy because the receiver is in the right place and ready.

# Year 2

# Lesson Plan 5 • 30 minutes
## January

**Emphasis on:** *(a) engaging vigorously in activities to keep warm; (b) co-operating with a partner to improve and extend skills.*

## Warm-up and Footwork Practices
### 5 minutes

1  Follow your leader, who will show you two or three lively actions to warm up the big muscles, particularly the legs. Can you copy these actions precisely? (Look out for, comment on and encourage jogging, sprinting, jumping, bouncing, hopping, skipping, leaping.)

2  Couples tag. Four couples start off as chasers. When one of the pair touches a dodger, the caught boy or girl changes place with the one who caught them to form a new chasing couple.

## Skills Practices: with a large ball — 10 minutes

### Individual practices

1  Carry ball in both hands like a rugby player. Run around and when I call 'Change!' place your ball down like a rugby player scoring a try, and pick up a different ball. Continue running and listening for my signal to 'Change!'

2  Throw ball up and forwards a short distance ahead of you. Run to catch with two hands near eye level.

### Partner practices

1  Jog, side by side, passing the ball, rugby fashion, a short distance in front of your partner to let him or her run and meet it each time. Use two hands and a lot of care.

2  Make two-handed chest and bounce passes to each other at about 3 metres apart. After every pass, move sideways and forwards to a new space to receive the return pass. Pass; move; receive.

## Group Practices
### 15 minutes

### Skipping rope each

On the spot, practise the slow double beat of feet for every turn of the rope, and the quicker single beat. Skip on the move and show me your best style of non-stop skipping. Direction changes are interesting.

### Five large balls among group of ten

Five with balls are dodging away from the others, who are trying to touch a ball to gain it. Rugby style game with ball carriers allowed to run, carrying in both hands. Touch ball gently, not the person.

### Large ball among four: 2 v 2; half pitch

Invent a 'three lives' game with one pair having three attacks to score. After defence steal ball three times, teams change duties. Decide how to score; one main rule to keep game going; and how to re-start after a goal.

**Games**

# Teaching notes and NC guidance
# Development over 4 lessons

## Warm-up and Footwork Practices

1 In mid-winter the class can be told about this first energetic activity while still in the classroom. Partners can be arranged and the action can start immediately they reach the play area. Stoppages for explanations or demonstrations will be kept to a minimum, and most of the teaching and praising takes place while the class is moving.

2 Couples tag keeps pupils moving vigorously in pursuit or dodging. It also keeps them thinking as the catcher breaks away from the pair and the newly caught pupil joins on. The game is stopped every 30 seconds or so to check on 'Who are the good dodgers, not caught at all?' and to introduce new chasers.

## Skills Practices: with a large ball

### Individual practices

1 Ball is carried in both hands with straight arms hanging low in front of you. With the rhythm of the running, the ball is gently swung from side to side. On 'Change!' ensure that the ball is placed, not dropped, with downward hands pressure, on to ground.

2 Throw up and forwards a short distance. Make throw high enough to allow a catch near eye level with two hands. Be sensible about the space you throw in to. Avoid others.

### Partner practices

1 Emphasise low carry of ball in front of you. Arms swing from side to side naturally. Keep body facing forwards while running, but twist upper body to face partner as you pass ball just ahead of him or her, high enough for a good mid-chest catch.

2 Chest pass is aimed at partner's chest. Bounce pass is aimed at ground about 1 metre in front of partner. After every pass, move to a new space, but still only about 3 metres apart. If 'Pass, then move! Give, then go! Pass, run to a space!' is emphasised at this age, the quality of team play, now and in the junior school, will be greatly improved.

## Group Practices

### Skipping rope each

Give them something to think about and plan while skipping on the spot or moving. Single- and double-beat foot action on the spot for slower or quicker skipping, with one or two bounces for each rope turn. On the move can be with feet together, or like running with one foot after the other.

### Five large balls among group of ten

Rugby ball touch is helped by pupils being allowed to run, holding the ball in a rugby style. Teacher can add interest by calling 'Change!' when all the carriers must put the ball on the ground and let the other half of the group become the dodgers.

### Large ball among four: 2 v 2; half pitch

Three lives' games played in one direction only have the same attackers and defenders until the defenders steal possession thrice. This allows two little games to be played in the one third. Teams need to decide the one main rule, the scoring method, and how to re-start after a score.

# Lesson Plan 6 • 30 minutes
## February

**Emphasis on:** *(a) showing increasing control over own movement; (b) linking movements to demonstrate increasing versatility.*

## Warm-up and Footwork Practices
### 5 minutes

1   Can you run and jump high, run and jump long over the lines and show me the difference? (High: at medium speed, rocking up on take-off foot, with leading bent knee reaching up. Long: at speed, with long, straight, leading leg well forwards.)

2   Teacher's space tag. Teacher and four helpers 'guard' the middle third of the playground, touching the remainder to prevent them scoring a point for a clear run to opposite side of third. Four helpers are changed over often.

## Skills Practices: with a skipping rope
### 10 minutes

### Individual practices

1   Choose one way to skip that you find easy. Can you all keep going for a whole minute, starting from... now!

2   Can you link together a way of skipping on the spot with one on the move, and keep alternating them?

### Partner practices

1   Place ropes on ground, side by side, about 1 metre apart. Can you make up a little balancing sequence along the ropes as a pair? (For example, one or both hands joined, balancing sideways, forwards or backwards; or facing in different directions.)

2   Watch your partner doing a favourite piece of skipping. Tell your partner what you liked about it. Change.

## Group Practices
### 15 minutes

### Large ball between two

Can you invent a 1 against 1, simple game, using one ball and part of a line? How will you score? What is main rule to keep game going? How will you re-start after a score? (For example, 1 v 1, to hand or foot dribble to cross line.)

### Partners with rope each

Play follow the leader, where the leader, 3 metres ahead, demonstrates at least two actions for a partner to copy. Watch your leader's feet, together or apart; and actions, walking, running, bouncing; and the directions.

### Hoop 'safe' tag with eight hoops

Three chasers wearing bands chase to touch the remainder, when they are not 'safe' in a hoop. Those who are caught take a band and become extra chasers. If dodgers 'hide' too long in hoops, teacher calls 'All move!' Gentle touches by chasers. No hard, dangerous pushing.

**Games**

# Teaching notes and NC guidance
# Development over 4 lessons

## Warm-up and Footwork Practices

1 For unimpeded, safe, continuous practice, pupils should be reminded to 'visit every part of the playground space, never following anyone' and not run in an anti-clockwise circle, typical of much primary school running, all following one another.

2 Because dodgers are running towards one another across the middle third, they must do so with great care to avoid head-on bumps. Dodgers should be using clever footwork such as direction changes and side steps, and not racing flat out.

## Skills Practices: with a skipping rope

### Individual practices

1 Easy skipping includes the slow overhead pull and the step over the rope sliding along the ground towards you; running action skipping with one foot leading over the rope; skipping on the spot, slowly, with a double beat of the feet for every swing over of the rope. (Jump and bounce.)

2 Progression in Physical Education includes moving on from simple and isolated movements to making short sequences of linked movements. Here we want skipping on the spot linked to skipping on the move.

### Partner practices

1 The words 'balancing sequence', which is the challenge here, mean that more than one way to balance must be planned and practised. One could be with hands joined, one without a join; facing same way could alternate with facing opposite ways.

2 Watching and commenting on a partner demonstration trains pupils in observing the elements of movement. What actions? What use of body parts? What directions? What speed? Saying something about it trains them in reflecting and evaluating, which are important requirements within the NC.

## Group Practices

### Large ball between two

In a specified, limited area, pupils are challenged to 'invent a competitive, 1 against 1 game'. They have to plan, decide and agree on the nature of the game; how to score within it; what is the one main rule; and how to restart after a goal or point has been scored.

### Partners with rope each

The follow-the-leader skipping sequence must have at least two parts to be a sequence, featuring linked actions. Apart from quality, of course, a good sequence includes variety and contrast, e.g. feet together, going sideways quickly, then running feet going forwards slowly.

### Hoop 'safe' tag with eight hoops

In hoop 'safe' tag, coloured bands are placed on the ground for the newly caught to pick up and wear as they join the other chasers. Particularly if the weather is cold, the dodgers should be told to 'Linger seldom. Move often' to keep warm and give chasers some activity in pursuing.

# Year 2

# Lesson Plan 7 • 30 minutes
## March

**Emphasis on:** *(a) varied activities possible with a hoop; (b) demonstrating enthusiastically when asked and watching others' demonstrations with interest and helpful comments.*

## Warm-up and Footwork Practices
### 5 minutes

1   Run quietly, following no-one. When I call 'Change!' change direction by pushing hard with one foot to stop your forwards movement and to make you go another way. Right foot firmly pressed on to ground pushes you off to the left, to run facing a new direction.

2   All-against-all tag, trying not to be caught by others. No hard, dangerous pushing. Touch gently. (Teacher checks best number caught by chasers, and fewest times caught by dodgers.) A sudden direction change is a good dodge.

## Skills Practices: with hoops
### 10 minutes

### Individual practices

1   Place all hoops on ground, well spaced out. Run and jump over some hoops and quickly step in and out of some hoops. Pretend some are obstacles and some are stepping stones. When I call 'Stop!' show me how quickly you can find a hoop to stand in. (Repeat.)

2   Can you walk forwards, either bowling your hoop, or doing low, two-handed little throws and catches? Share the space sensibly and don't bump or throw towards others.

3   There are many ways to skip using a hoop, including skipping around it, while on the ground; using one or two hands, forwards and back, side to side, or diagonally; swinging low; or overhead like a skipping rope. Show me what you can do.

## Group Practices
### 15 minutes

### Partners, with a quoit: 1 against 1

Make the quoit go over a long rope 'net' tied between chairs or netball posts. Decide how to start and score; one main rule to keep game going; and how many points in a game.

### Hoop each

Try spinning the hoop on the ground, ankle, wrist or waist. Jog beside your hoop, bowling gently with one hand across top of hoop. Can you spin the hoop to make it come back to you?

### Large ball among four: 2 v 2; end line touch

Play in half of your area with several ways agreed to score, e.g. touch end line; bounce in one of hoops in the corners; pass to partner on end line. Decide a main rule to keep game going, and how to re-start.

**Games**

# Teaching notes and NC guidance
## Development over 4 lessons

## Warm-up and Footwork Practices

1  Pupils have been changing direction in every Games lesson, but probably without thinking about the technique involved. Here we are consciously stopping the forward movement by pressing down hard on one foot which also then sends us off with a strong push into the new direction. A lean of the upper body into the new line is helpful.

2  In all-against-all tag, encourage practice of sudden direction changes to evade a chaser following or coming towards you. For safety's sake, insist on 'Gentle touching only so that no-one is knocked down and hurt.'

## Skills Practices: with hoops

### Individual practices

1  All 30 hoops being used in the lesson are well spaced out, with ten in each third. Some are placed just close enough to act as 'stepping stones'. A rhythmic pattern is possible. 'Jump over; jump over; step and step and step.'

2  In bowling, walk beside your hoop with your fingers across it, pointing away from you, just below the top. Pull with your hand to try to roll it forwards. In throwing and catching, with both hands wrapped around the hoop, close together, the hands open and close, keeping some contact throughout.

3  Skipping with a slow, short, one-handed swing from side to side is like skipping over a low rope swinging from side to side, and is the easiest to start with, before progressing on to two-handed swing overhead. Two bounces of the feet to each rope swing are recommended.

## Group Practices

### Partners, with a quoit: 1 against 1

In competitive, 1-against-1 quoits, you score if the quoit lands on the ground on your opponent's side of the rope 'net', which is at head height. One hand is used for throwing and two are used for catching. Some chalk marks for the side of each little 'court' are recommended, to contain the game.

### Hoop each

Free practice with a hoop allows more time to practise the skills performed or seen earlier in the lesson and to try out some of the teacher's challenges. 'Can you...?'

### Large ball among four

Played in half of a third of the teaching space, 2 v 2 with a large ball aims to encourage each pair to keep possession and to try to advance themselves and the ball to score in ways that they agree. More ways to score make the defending pair space apart more to cover, for example, the end line and the two hoops. Spreading the defenders gives the attackers more room and more chances to score. In this game we hope that the players will decide: how to score, often using more than one way; how to re-start after a score; the one main rule that helps to keep the game going.

# Lesson Plan 8 • 30 minutes
## April

**Emphasis on:** *(a) showing good planning in safe, appropriate solutions to tasks; (b) demonstrating good control over body, good sharing of space, and good footwork to be in the right place at the right time.*

## Warm-up and Footwork Practices
### 5 minutes

1   Can you mix quick walking, easy jogging and short bursts of sprinting as you use the whole playground carefully and safely? In jogging, heels and arms are carried low. In your sprints, lift heels and knees strongly.

2   Count how many two-footed jumps you need to cross from one side line to the opposite side line. Use your arms strongly to pull you far forwards. Swing them forwards, then back with a bend of the knees, then swing them forwards and spring from both feet.

## Skills Practices: with short-tennis rackets and ball
### 10 minutes

### Individual practices

1   Can you bounce the ball continuously up from your racket? Use a gentle wrist action with racket held near eye level.

2   Can you bounce your ball continuously down on to the ground? Try this standing, then slowly moving forwards, still using the wrist action only. No hard hitting with elbow or shoulder.

3   Throw ball up straight to let it bounce up. Hit it up, let it bounce, catch it with non-hitting hand and start again. What is your best score of controlled hitting and catching?

### Partner practices

1   Throw ball to partner who strikes it back for an easy catch. Hit it gently and change over after five catches.

2   Both with a racket now, can you very gently keep the ball bouncing once only, between hits, as you hit low and slow to each other? Start by dropping the ball, letting it bounce up, then sending it. Stand about 4–5 metres apart only, and be gentle.

## Group Practices
### 15 minutes

### Ten hoops on ground

Invent a chasing and dodging game, using the hoops and keeping inside your own area. Chasers wear bands. Decide the main rule, how players are caught, what to do when caught.

### Short-tennis racket each

Practise by yourself to improve your ball and racket control. You can practise on the spot, hitting up, down or a mixture. Moving, you can hit up, down and from side to side.

### Large ball among four

Team passing with 3 against 1. The 3 try to keep the ball and make passes. 1 tries to 'steal' the ball by vigorous chasing after the ball. 1 can be passive if passing is not good and needs help.

**Games**

# Teaching notes and NC guidance
# Development over 4 lessons

## Warm-up and Footwork Practices

1  'Easy' jogging is done with an upright body, small steps, arms and heels carried low, and is easier than quick walking. The sprinting strides are rapid, with hands and heels carried higher, and are tiring and space consuming, so should be done in short bursts through spaces where others are not impeded.

2  A series of standing, two-footed jumps is performed with each jump starting at the place where the previous one landed. Feet apart with toes turned in slightly; a long arm swing forwards, then back with a knee bend, and forwards strongly with the dynamic stretch of the legs; and a low layout in flight, all help the jump to be as long as possible.

## Skills Practices: with short-tennis rackets and ball

### Individual practices

1  Racket is held near its face, not near the end of its handle, to give better control, and it is held near the chest so that the ball can be watched closely.

2  Because the racket is springy, pupils do not need to apply much force when batting the ball down to bounce up to waist height for the next hit down. We want them to 'feel' how much or how little force is needed. Beginners usually hit too hard.

3  Throwing up; letting bounce; hitting straight up; and catching are another example of 'performing simple skills and joining them together with increasing control', as required within the NC.

## Partner practices

1  If ball is bounced about 1 metre in front of batter and comes up to just above waist height, the batter has an easy return to the bowler, whose hands should be cupped and forwards, ready.

2  In hitting very gently to each other, pupils should again aim to bounce the ball 1 metre in front of partner to give him or her the best possible chance to return it. 'Low and slow' to land for an easy return, ideally from partner's forehand, is the aim.

## Group Practices

### Ten hoops on ground

With ten inventing and playing a chasing and dodging game, the teacher might initially suggest three chasers wearing bands who can catch you if you are not in a hoop, 'safe' and untouchable. This will give the game a start from which other suggestions will follow from the pupils, e.g. when caught, take a band and become a chaser; 'hiding' in the hoop to be no more than 5 seconds long.

### Short-tennis racket each

Racket skills are the most difficult and seldom practised away from school. Personal practice aims to reinforce the work done earlier in the lesson with individual coaching by the teacher.

### Large ball among four

Team passing, 3 against 1, is a most important practice for our traditional invasion/running games, such as netball, football, hockey and basketball, to encourage running to a space to be available for a return pass, well away from opponents.

# Lesson Plan 9 • 30 minutes
## May

**Emphasis on:** *(a) running, jumping, throwing and skipping; (b) practising to improve performance; (c) dependence on a partner to provide the unpredictable situations so often found in Games*

## Warm-up and Footwork Practices
### 5 minutes

1 Follow your leader who will show you some actions as you run and jump. For example, hurdling, scissors jumping, long and high jumps, and two-footed take-off long jumps.

2 Side-line sprints. Couples stand side by side down the centre of the area. On the signal 'Go!' each sprints to the nearer side line, touches it with a foot and races back to touch partner's hand. A signal 'Four!' or 'Six!', for example, will start a race where pupils sprint to the line and touch it four or six times.

## Skills Practices — with a small ball

### Individual practices

1 Throw up and catch with two hands at eye level. Now do the same thing, walking and keeping an eye on the ball.

2 Walk forwards, throwing ball up to bounce in front of you. Catch it after the bounce.

3 Can you walk, batting the ball down on to the ground with left and right hands?

### Partner practices

1 One partner throws straight for other to catch. Second partner bounces it back. Change over after six.

2 Roll ball for partner to ground, field, pick up and roll back.

3 Stand on opposite sides of a line, about 3 metres from the line. Throw, aiming to hit the line and give partner a catch.

## Group Practices
### 15 minutes

### Partners: skittle and a small ball

Bowl to bounce up to hit skittle. Partner is wicket keeper who throws or rolls ball back. Have six goes each and change over, keeping your own best score. Can you work out where a 'good length bounce' would land?

### Partners: skipping rope each

Can you show me some examples of what we might call 'partner skipping'? You can use own rope and follow the leader, or watch each other's favourite practice. You can try to skip together, using one rope only.

### Hand tennis over line or rope 'net'

Serve by dropping ball, letting it bounce up, and then striking it to land on partner's side of net. Decide the one main rule to keep the game fair and going. How many points in a game before changing ends?

**Games**

# Teaching notes and NC guidance
# Development over 4 lessons

## Warm-up and Footwork Practices

**1** May is an appropriate month for using athletics terminology and explaining and showing, for example, hurdling, scissors jumping, and long and high jumping. In hurdling over lines approached from the front, we swing up and down with a straight leading leg and a trailing leg that lifts out and to the side, then forwards. A scissors jump from an angle swings the nearer leg up and over the line.

**2** In side-line sprints, everyone starts on the signal. They must touch their own side line and their own partner. Cheating must be looked out for and strongly objected to, so that the winners are the true winners.

## Skills Practices: with a small ball

### Individual practices

**1** Class can all stand, throwing and catching with two hands at eye level, so that teacher can check hand positions and height thrown. If this is satisfactory, they practise on the move, with well-cupped hands and eyes looking closely at the ball.

**2** A throw up and forwards, with a swing back and forwards with a long arm, aims to go just high enough and far enough forwards for the next bounce to come up nicely ahead of you for a catch.

**3** Continuous batting downwards, 'as in basket-ball', is usually done well by this age group, and is easier with a hand than with a bat or racket. A gentle wrist action is all that is needed.

### Partner practices

**1** At a distance apart of 3 metres, one throws straight to the partner's outstretched hands in front of chest with a long underarm aiming action. The other partner throws a bounce return with ball starting high above the shoulder, and aiming to land it 1 metre in front of partner, for a chest-height catch.

**2** Still 3 metres apart, they roll ball for partner to crouch to field with both hands behind the ball, with fingers facing down.

**3** Aiming to hit a line between you and your partner is done with a high starting position with ball above shoulder.

## Group Practices

### Partners: skittle and a small ball

Bowler aims underarm to land in front of wicket skittle to bounce up to hit it. The many which miss this difficult target will be fielded by the wicket keeper who rolls ball back to the bowler.

### Partners: skipping rope each

Year 2 partner skipping produces a most interesting variety of work, as the pupils approach the end of their year. The work deserves to be demonstrated as a way of expanding the class repertoire, and the teacher's repertoire. Skipping together, using one rope only, is now achievable by some.

### Hand tennis over line or rope 'net'

For this competitive 1-against-1 hand tennis game over a long rope 'net', they need to agree on: how to serve; how to score; and any allowances to make to keep the game going and fair.

# Lesson Plan 10 • 30 minutes
### June

**Emphasis on:** *(a) variety from individual, partner and group activities; (b) variety from running, skipping, throwing and striking a ball; (c) variety from planning, doing, reflecting and commenting.*

## Warm-up and Footwork Practices
### 5 minutes

1 With a partner, run side by side at the same speed. Each has a turn at setting the rhythm of the running. Run in good style, with good lifting of heels and knees, and with whole body 'straight ahead'.

2 Jumping alternately, see how few standing long jumps your partner and you need to take you from side line to opposite side line. One jumps and stands still in landing place. Two starts behind toe line of one and does his or her standing, two-footed long jump. Count how many (or few) jumps you needed. Try to improve on the way back by really driving hard and long into your strong leap.

## Skills Practices: with a skipping rope
### 10 minutes

### Individual practices

1 Can you link together two or three ways of skipping, including one on the spot and one on the move?

2 Choose one way you enjoy skipping and find easy to keep going. Let me see if the whole class can be brilliant and keep going for a minute. Ready?... Begin!

### Partner practices

1 With ropes placed parallel on the ground, can you make up a little balancing sequence along the ropes, as a pair (e.g. side by side or facing each other; one or both hands joined; balance walk forwards, sideways or backwards)?

2 Can you remind each other of some examples of the 'partner skipping' you tried last month? Practise again and try to do something using one rope only.

## Group Practices
### 15 minutes

### Groups of four: short-tennis racket or small bat and ball

Two with two tennis over a long rope 'net' tied between chairs. Co-operate to keep a long rally going and keep your best score without a stoppage.

### Skipping rope each

Can your whole group practise to show the class a group demonstration of varied skipping – ones, pairs, on the spot and moving, fast and slow, feet together and apart?

### Large ball among four in half of area

Can you invent a game for four players, using one ball and the lines around your area? How will you score? What will be your main rule to keep the game fair and going?

**Games**

# Teaching notes and NC guidance
# Development over 4 lessons

## Warm-up and Footwork Practices

1 Partners running at the same 'cruising' speed should 'feel' the repeating rhythm that is being quietly sounded out by their feet. It should be slow enough to allow a good lifting of knees, heels, arms and head. Keep together, one, two, three, four!

2 In a standing-start broad jump, start with feet slightly apart with toes turned in a little way. Swing both arms forwards high, back with a good knees bend, and forwards hard as you do your reach into your long jump. Pull both feet forwards to land.

## Skills Practices: with a skipping rope

### Individual practices

1 Skipping on the spot and on the move mixes the more demanding actions on the spot with the physically easier ones while on the move. We can challenge pupils, 'Can you skip with feet together then moving one after the other?' or 'Can you turn the rope to the front while you travel backwards?' or 'Can you include one quick jump for each turn, then the slower two jumps for each turn?'

2 Skipping inspires leg-muscle action, which inspires heart and lungs action, leading to improved fitness. Many primary-school children express an interest in becoming fitter and they can test themselves by trying to keep going for a minute's skipping, which is something they can then practise at home.

## Partner practices

1 Ask pupils to try some of the many ways that a pair can join for balancing with a support. As well as both facing the same way, they can have one going forwards, one going backwards. Tell them to 'Feel for the rope with each foot before putting your weight down. Feel for it. Do not look down for it.'

2 Partner skipping can include: following the leader; one watching, the other copying; a mirroring sequence that changes after an agreed number of repetitions; or the difficult pair skipping with only one rope, held by one or both.

## Group Practices

### Groups of four: short-tennis racket or small bat and ball

Co-operative tennis over a low rope 'net' to 'Find your best score as a group. Can you keep going for six good hits? Ask them to move early to be in position for the return hit, ideally in a 'side-on' position. Start by dropping the ball for a good bounce up to hit.

### Skipping rope each

Emphasise that each rope group will give a demonstration to show variety, quality, and excellent shared use of space, and to increase the class skipping repertoire. Look out for and comment on: on the spot and moving; different directions and speeds; solo and duo; varied actions in feet and legs.

### Large ball among four in half of area

With one large ball among four, the eventual game invented will probably have 2 v 2, or 1 v 3; will be played in half of the group's area; and will need one main rule and a scoring system.

# Lesson Plan 11 • 30 minutes
## July

**Emphasis on:** *(a) planning and performing safely a range of simple actions and linked movements in response to given tasks; (b) demonstrating improvements, generally, in performances that are accurate, consistent and look 'easy'; (c) reflecting competently in pointing out key features and expressing pleasure after observing a performance.*

## Warm-up and Footwork Practices
### 5 minutes

1   Jog easily, 'coasting' along at a speed which you think you can maintain almost as easily as quick walking. In your jogging, arms and heels are lower than in stylish or fast running. Can you 'feel' this rhythm which you find easy to continue?

2   Cross-court relays. Partners stand, side by side, down the middle of the area. On 'Go!' one partner sprints to touch his or her nearer side line, then sprints back to touch partner's outstretched hand. Second partner sprints to own, nearer side line, then back to touch first partner's hand. This continues until the pair have made the number of touches asked for, when the teacher tries to call out the results.

## Skills Practices: with a small ball and bat
### 5 minutes

### Partner practices

1   Batting partner, strike the ball from one hand, high, to give partner an easy catch. Catcher, roll the ball back to your partner. Have six goes then change.

2   Batting partner, strike ball along ground to give partner fielding practice. Fielder, send ball back to batter with one bounce for an easy, one-handed catch. Have six goes and then change.

3   French cricket. Bowler aims ball to hit partner on the leg below knee height, from about 2 metres away, slowly and gently. Batter guards legs with bat held low and turns ball away. Fielder next throws from where he or she picked up the ball. (Game is kept contained by insisting on gentle aiming and hitting.) Change when bowler hits legs of batter.

## Group Practices
### 20 minutes

### Long rope in groups of four

Two take turns at swinging the rope low from side to side. Skippers try to come in, skip several times, then move away from the still swinging rope.

### 4 v 4: three-catch rounders

Batting team has one innings each, striking ball to land in the limited area being used. Batters all follow hitter around the diamond of three skittles. Fielders make three catches and shout 'Stop!' Batters score one run for each skittle.

### Partners: short tennis; 1 v 1

A competitive game played over a line or rope 'net'. Decide how to serve to start game, and how to score. How many points in a game before changing ends?

**Games**

# Teaching notes and NC guidance
# Development over 4 lessons

## Warm-up and Footwork Practices

1  Easy jogging has lower arms and heels than normal athletic, good-style running. The steps are shorter and there is a feeling of a continuing rhythm, which the runner should be able to feel: 'Jog; jog; easy; easy. One, two, three, four. One, two, three four.'

2  In cross-court relays, emphasise that they touch just over the line, each time, with a foot. Also, they must wait to be touched by the incoming partner. (The over-competitive touch short of the line, and go before being touched.) A crouched, sprint-start position by the second runner gets him or her off to a more explosive start.

## Skills Practices: with a small bat and ball

### Partner practices

1  Ball is struck from hand as in a table-tennis service. Striker should be side-on to receiving partner. 3 metres apart is an easy distance and sufficient for receiver to see ball's speed and flight, and react. 'Keep your best team score of good hits and catches out of 12.'

2  Batter tries to send the ball along ground, without bouncing, for partner to field with both hands and body behind ball. Hands are spread wide with fingers down towards ground, and small fingers can be crossed to 'make a floor for the basket made by the hands'.

3  In French cricket, make it a main rule that the ball stays in the limited area the pair is using. In other words, 'No big hits!' Bowler is enouraged to bowl underarm at a good length, to land ball about half a metre in front of the batter's legs, which are the target. Batter plays a purely defensive stroke to push the ball away 2 or 3 metres to what is the next bowling position.

## Group Practices

### Long rope in groups of four

In long-rope skipping in fours where two swing and two skip, the rope swingers only swing the rope from side to side, if the skippers are learners. With more expert performers the rope is swung in a complete circle. Both learners and experts move in to skip as the rope swings away from them (i.e. in from left as rope swings up to right). They leave rope one way as it swings the other (i.e. out to left as rope moves to right).

### 4 v 4: three-catch rounders

In 4-against-4 rounders, the main rule is that the ball must not leave the area allocated. When each one of batting team has had one hit, the teams change over. The three catches of the fielding team must involve three different players. Bowler is asked to bowl underarm to let ball bounce about 1 metre in front of the batter. A bat or a hand can be used for the striking to enable easy hitting.

### Partners: short tennis; 1 v 1

The competitive, 1-against-1 short tennis over a long, low rope 'net' can be better contained if chalk marks are made at the sides of each little 'court'. The easiest serve is to drop the ball to make it bounce straight up to be hit at about mid-chest height. Encourage pupils to stand 'side-on' to their opponents, with the chest facing to one side, not towards the opponent.